GIVING FORM NANCY
TO FEELING KING

Giving  Form To Feeling

 **NANCY KING**

Drama Book Specialists [Publishers]
New York

Library of Congress Cataloging in Publication Data

King, Nancy, 1936-
   Giving form to feeling.

   1. Creative thinking (Education) I. Title.
LB1062.K48   370.15′2   74-23359
ISBN 0-910482-57-8

Printed in the United States of America

10 9 8 7 6 5 4

For
  Lance King
and
  Didde Hannover
  Becky Hannover
and
  Evan Matteo

Table of Contents

Section III

Preface

Recently, a teacher came up to me during a workshop I was leading and told me that what had happened to her that day in class:

"The damage was done, and there was no point in yelling, but I was bursting with anger, and needed some release. I didn't know what to do, so I told everybody to return to their work, but that didn't serve any purpose. No-one could concentrate, nothing was communicated; we merely went through the motions of learning."

The teacher in this case was about 40 years old, had received traditional training, and had been teaching for over ten years. Yet she was still unsatisfied with her ability to deal with certain problems of emotion and communication in the classroom; she often felt herself coming up against walls. She said to me, "I wish you would write down some of your activities and suggestions. Then, when I have the time, or if I am in trouble, I would have a book to refer to, which would help me out of difficult situations." *Giving Form to Feeling* is my response.

We all give form to feeling. But it is necessary to be aware of the great variety of forms that can express feelings, and to be able to deal openly with feelings. The activities in this book provide teachers and students with the opportunity to explore different forms, and see the effects of this exploration on stimulating imagination and on expressing this in relationships with people.

Whether studying fine arts, languages or sciences, the process of exploration remains the same. A teacher needs no special background to do these activities; all that is required is an openness to different responses, and a willingness to experiment. Once a teacher understands this process, he or she will be able to develop new activities, based on individual and group needs. Thinking of questions and new activities will develop an aesthetic awareness and new bases for critical evaluation. The activities in this book and similar ones will help improve verbal and non-verbal communication, the access to imagination and feelings, and the ability to express these feelings.

I would appreciate hearing from people about their own activities. A second edition, including this material, might be warranted. Please send any suggestions to:

Nancy King
Department of Dramatic Arts
University of Delaware
Newark, Delaware 19711

1

questioning

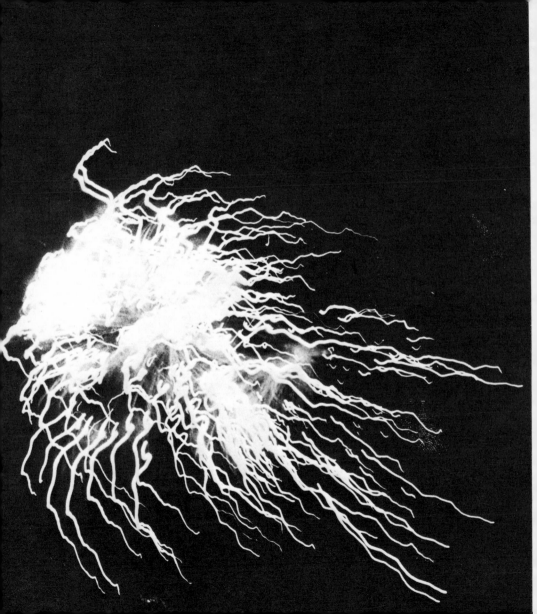

Festivity and fantasy are not only worthwhile in themselves; they are absolutely vital to human life. They enable man to relate himself to the past and the future . . . If festivity enables man to enlarge his experience by reliving events of the past, fantasy is a form of play that extends the frontiers of the future . . .

If he is to survive, man must be both innovative and adaptive. He must draw from the richest wealth of experience available to him, and must never be bound to existing formulas for solving problems . . . Together, festivity and fantasy enable man to experience his present in a richer, more joyful and more creative way.

Harvey Cox,
Feast of Fools.
Cambridge, Mass.:
Harvard University Press, 1969.

It is generally accepted that children have fertile imaginations. At a remarkably early age, however, due to conditions at home and school, the creative and imaginative impulses are often stifled, along with the ability to express ideas and feelings. This is partially the fault of teaching methods which discourage students from asking questions and seeking multiple solutions, and encourage following narrow, prescribed lines of thought, requiring rote memorization. The purpose of this book is to help teachers as well as students regain access to, and develop the imagination, so it is possible to look at something and describe not only what it *is* but also what it *could be*.

It is difficult to apply value judgements to imaginative work, since all responses are equally valid for each individual. As such, imaginative work serves as a force for democratization. It also is self-generating and perpetuating, since sharing ideas and feelings offers new material for further exploration.

Very little is known about optimal conditions for learning. It is known, however, that strain hinders and relaxation helps; it is also known that poorly structured criticism causes defensiveness and tension, closing the student off. A good environment would be one in which students were free to respond spontaneously and openly, without fear of premature judgement. The activities in this book provide teachers and students, sharing common experiences, with the opportunity to explore relationships, imagination, and expression. In an environment that supports and encourages questioning, people will become aware of their own

feelings and the feelings of others, and will be able to give form to
these feelings.

What does "giving form to feeling" mean?

Our feelings, attitudes and ideas are with us, no matter what we
do. They often interfere, and transform what we want to happen,
creating difficult problems. Giving form to feeling enables a person to identify and use feelings in personally rewarding and
socially acceptable ways. Denying an angry person's right to
anger serves no purpose; the energy of anger remains. Often an
angry person lets this energy out by hitting, shouting, cursing or
provoking further interaction. None of this usually provides
adequate release, so people try to conceal anger at great personal
expense. Even young children develop ulcers, rashes and muscle
tension. Ideally, an angry person would acknowledge the feeling,
and find constructive ways to make the energy work. Other
emotions may also be difficult to express; often feelings of love or
joy create large pools of energy because outlets are difficult to
find.

Learning to identify the feeling is only the beginning. Then it
is necessary to be aware of other people's feelings, and learn how
to work with them. Ultimately, feelings will combine with intellect in a total response. For example, in studying the role of
immigration in the development of the United States, students
should consider the following type of questions: What would a
person need to feel before leaving the known for the unknown?
How might these feelings have developed? How would it feel to

live in a strange country where no one spoke your language? How would parents feel if their children learned the new language while they still were having difficulty? What are the expectations, and what happens when they are not fulfilled? Such questions integrate feelings and intellect, and create a richer educational experience.

What formal training is required?

I ask this question because it is so often asked of me. My answer is: None. Where you are is where you start.

There are many ways that you can prepare for this work, and in training yourself you will experience the same process as your students. Technical training in the arts helps, but is not enough; a willingness to be open and experiment imaginatively is needed. Preparation and execution of activities is sometimes difficult because of shyness, embarrassment, lack of self-confidence or feeling uncreative, but these can be overcome.

Think about why you want to use this program. Perhaps because you know your students will benefit; perhaps because you need a new way of working. These reasons will get you through doubts and discouragements. If the program increases communication between you and your students, or between the students and others, this reward will stimulate further exploration.

There are many ways to prepare. Try as many of the activities as possible by yourself and with family and friends. Keep a diary of your reactions. Sometimes, work spontaneously, rather than with a predetermined plan. Ask yourself: What do I really want to do today? What pleases me? What upsets me? How else could I have reponded? Set aside a time in each day to do something which is pleasurable. Notice what interests you, what you would like to try.

Present an activity with which you are unfamiliar: How do you feel? Is it valuable? When I present unfamiliar material which I would like to learn more about, my group becomes very supportive and explores possibilities with me. They become more open about problems and questions. Try to structure your classroom so that you become less and less the center of authority, taste and judgement; help your students make their own decisions about their work.

Encourage another teacher to work in a similar program. Even if the results differ, sharing the experience will help you both maintain perspective. Deciding how the program works for you will suggest how it helps your students.

Try to be aware of your tensions so you can deal with them. Try to communicate what and how you feel. Explore sensory awareness by doing the following: When tired, stretch your whole body; first by yourself, and then with another person. Massage your face and feet. Experiment with paints and paper. Do you feel comfortable or self-conscious? Would you feel better if you worked to music? Work with clay. Can your fingers decide what shapes will emerge? Taste foods before looking at them. Notice how many sounds you can hear in a quiet room. How many smells do you encounter on your way to work? Try cooking without a recipe. Watch television without the sound, to focus on non-verbal communication. Go to a movie in a foreign language.

Exercises in extending sensitivity will encourage other questions, such as: How involved in the present are you? Do you spend most of your time thinking, "I can't wait until Friday" or "I wish I had behaved differently at the party last night"? Try not to worry about things which are out of your control. If this is difficult, analyze why you want to worry. What happens when you make a list of all your worries?

Avoid saying *cannot*, *will not* or *should* for a period of time; how does this affect you? Ask yourself what choices you have. Do you explore the alternatives? In difficult situations, ask yourself: What is the worst that could happen? Is it really so terrible? Are you realistic in your assessment? How does confronting your feelings affect your actions?

These exercises, as well as the questions they generate, are not very effective if you do them once and then forget about them. Continue to work on them over a long period of time.

Why use the Arts?

The arts are a tool to facilitate the expression of feelings; they offer experiences which can be explored initially without concern for technique or rules. Writing, moving, painting, sculpting, singing, making sounds and doing drama are all ways of responding to particular situations. These activities should be done for the pleasure and understanding they bring to their participants; pedestals, frames, applause or other formal evaluations are irrelevant. Using feelings in work in the arts allows everybody to participate as equals; the teacher does not have to be more competent than the students to encourage artistic exploration.

Also, when using the arts, common definitions of failure and success do not apply; there are many solutions to any given problem. What appears as chaos is often an ordered search for variety. Within this potentially wide scope, participants can experience their own uniqueness, seeing the best and the worst in themselves. Students and teachers will be able to establish different working relationships which could be useful in other areas.

Finally, the arts develop skills and abilities that will serve students long after formal schooling ends. Those who find release or stimulation from a particular art form will be able to develop and enjoy it the rest of their lives.

2

my own beginnings

The child first tastes freedom when it realizes that it can say *NO* to its father; the slave, to its master; the subject, when he discovers that he can say *NO* to his king. But in every instance the newly liberated man soon becomes aware that freedom is more than a breaking of chains, that with emancipation the real tasks begin, that he has lost the guardianship of the protector and the comfort of a set of rules. Thus, early men discovered what their descendants were to discover over and over again: that winning "freedom from"—namely, authority—is only the first step, and that it is followed by the necessity to decide on a "freedom to"—a commitment.

Joseph B. Fabry,
The Pursuit of Meaning.
New York: Beacon Press, 1968.

A child who grows up in two different worlds learns very early that there is no one "right" way of doing anything, and that for every action there are at least two different reactions. This is the way it was for me.

My home was a world of books, concerts, theatre, eating in foreign restaurants, political activisim and concern for social equality. Questions asked were answered with new questions. A common response to a statement was "How do you know?" My parents, born of immigrants and raised in a ghetto, were constantly encouraging me to discover my limits and then go beyond them. Resting was for the sick, weak or very old. There were always new things to learn, experiences to try and people to get to know; my parents' energy and enthusiasm kept pushing me on.

Outside my home, both at school and at play, there was a world of people who were afraid of difference, searched for limits, avoided questions, and craved security and acceptance at any price. At school I was expected to keep my mouth shut, to keep my ideas to myself, and to worry about perfect attendance records. It was difficult to find friends to play with when I was the only one in my neighborhood who was not limited to riding my bike close to home, the only one who could make my own rules, and who spent most Saturdays at music and dance classes.

Although I felt that my world at home was better than the world of school, I still had to function in both simultaneously. There were no bridges between them. I learned to survive by accepting the fact that being different brought its own rewards, that finding my own way developed resourcefulness and strength. Often I was forced to act out of desperation; this appeared to be, and finally became, courage. I gradually accepted myself for who and what I was, and began to see my own painful growing experiences in terms of what they taught me and what I could share with others. This book has grown out of what I learned, how I learned it, and shows how teachers, parents, counselors and students can use the activities. Growth is often difficult, but if ways can be found to use negative experiences, then the memory of pain is transformed, and the experience can be viewed in a different, more constructive light. In my case, maturity meant the ability to confront myself and my experiences, to accept and use them. There is continuing exhilaration in this liberating process.

In the fourth grade, I read a book about an experiment in education in a school in Springfield, Massachusetts. The book showed how the teachers had developed a curriculum based on the *children's* ideas and questions, which impressed me as an exciting and new kind of education. When the teacher of my class assigned book reports, I prepared an oral report on this book, including pictures, anecdotes, and questions of my own about our educational system. I was about half-way through my report when the teacher stopped me, and asked me in a puzzled and angry tone if I had found my book in the children's section of the library. I said no, that I had taken it from the Education section. She motioned for me to sit down, and chastised me, saying, "This is not a suitable book for fourth graders to read. We are only interested in books appropriate for your age group."

Crushed, I returned to my seat, not hearing her say that I might have another chance. It took me many years to realize that perhaps the teacher's judgement, not mine, had been at fault.

I keep this incident in mind when I am about to comment on a child's work. It is so easy for a teacher to destroy confidence, enthusiasm and interest; often this happens without the teacher even realizing it.

Most of my philosophy of education comes from the experiences I had at a special junior high school. Here, innovative teachers, freedom to develop curricula based on students' questions, and special projects were the rule, not the exception. We were encouraged to visit the United Nations to interview foreign diplomats, to participate in the creation of plays and puppet shows, to visit museums, and to attend performances of all the arts. Our ideas were challenged, our abilities extended. This experience showed me that school could be as stimulating and creative as the one in the book I had read in the fourth grade.

Unfortunately, this ended when I entered high school. Teachers were no longer concerned with questions; the emphasis was on facts to be memorized, and exams to be passed. My interest in school revived when the academic work was finished, and extracurricular activities began.

My high school was overcrowded, so I and a few others were chosen and trained to help teach large gym classes. We directed 75 to 100 of our classmates in dance, sports and swimming. This experience served me well when I went to college which, for me, had to be inexpensive and away from home. Based on the teaching I did while in high school, I selected a college that, at the very least, prepared me to earn a living as a teacher of physical education. My education courses taught how to organize classes, how to structure lesson plans, and how to coach; but the professors never encouraged questions, never offered alternatives. I soon acquired the reputation of being rebellious and antagonistic.

In one of my education courses, I spent the entire semester of practice-teaching without one written lesson plan, to test and prove that there were other ways to prepare than the rigid, step-by-step approach. The night before my teaching diary was due, I stayed up all night typing mythical lesson plans, making fictional comments, problems and solutions. I was amused when I received my grades: "A" for "thorough and well-prepared lesson plans," and "B" for the diary, with a "B+" as the overall grade. The experience proved that there were many kinds of effective preparation. My search for alternative methods continues, which adds interest not only for my students but also for me; we constantly explore what did or did not work, and why.

Often, good methods of teaching evolve accidentally or circumstantially. One example of this occurred while in my third year of college. Even then it was difficult for me to justify my actions, but I avoided thinking about them until the incident passed.

I was fulfilling one of the requirements for the title of Water Safety Instructor, which required teaching a young child to swim. The student assigned to me was a thin, frightened seven-year old girl with a severe limp, the result of polio. Each instructor had seven sessions of thirty minutes to teach the child how to float, using arms and legs to keep off the bottom of the pool. I was eager to teach someone how to swim, and set off for the locker room full of confidence. I picked my student out right away; she was the only one not wearing a bathing suit. Unable to find her suit, I was somewhat shaken at not being able to get her into the pool. We ended up spending the first session in the locker room; I regaled her with stories about how much fun it was to swim. She seemed responsive until I mentioned going near the pool.

As she was leaving, she said she would remember her suit next time, which reassured me until I noticed something which closely resembled a swimsuit sticking out of the paper bag she had in her hand. Her eyes focusing directly on mine prevented me from asking the question. I was discouraged, but comforted myself with the thought that we had gotten to know each other a little, and that the next session would be better.

It was not. Nor the five that followed. By the end of the sixth week, I had finally gotten her to put on her suit and stand near the pool door. I was embarrassed, angry, and without inspiration. Several times I thought of asking the advice of another student, or of getting help from my instructor, but I was stopped by my feelings of self-pity. Instead of being aware of and dealing with the child's fear, I focused on my bad luck.

For the rest of the sessions we continued to tell stories and talk. Finally, the last day of class came, when the students would be tested. The other teachers and their students greeted each other eagerly. My student and I were quiet, sharing a difficult time. Resigned, I told her: "There's no point in putting on your suit. I'm sorry that I couldn't help you to swim, but there's no time left now to try. I'll tell my instructor that I was unable to teach you, and we can go for a soda." Even at this point I was thinking of myself. She was quiet for a moment and then asked, "What happens to you if you don't teach me to swim?" I was too miserable to be less than honest. "I'll have to wait until next year, and take this course over again; maybe then I'll do a better job." Incredulously, she asked, "You mean you fail the course because I can't swim?" "No," I replied, "I fail because I couldn't teach you to swim." In the long silence that followed, I think I looked at her for the first time, and saw the fear and sadness in her face. I hugged her, saying "It's OK, I know you wanted to help. It's not so terrible to fail. Next time I'll know more." She disagreed: "No, it's not OK. You shouldn't have to fail because of me. You told me all those stories; I should do something for you. Let's go to the pool."

I told her she didn't have to, but she moved away and started to put on her suit. I was overwhelmed by her anxiety, her caring for me, and my own selfishness. Switching roles, she led me into the pool room. She found a quiet corner in the shallow end and asked me "What do I do?" Looking at her small trembling body, I promised myself I would be less self-concerned the next time. Inspired by her determination and the disappearance of my tension, I directed her: "Put your face in the water, blow bubbles, do a dead man's float and then swim a little, using your arms and legs." We had ten minutes to do what we had been unable to do in seven sessions.

I heard and saw no one except her, although there were at least forty people in the pool. Our eyes left each other only when her face was in the water. Holding on tightly to my hand, she put her face in the water, blew some bubbles, and managed to float. My instructor came over, suprised to see us both in the water. She said to my student: "Show me what you can do by yourself." I got in the water, gave her my most encouraging smile, and watched, awestruck, as she managed about four strokes with her feet off the pool floor, propelling herself with her limbs. I could not contain myself. I rushed over and gave her an enormous hug, laughing and crying at the same time. "You did it!" I cried. She replied, "I didn't want you to fail because of me."

Later I understood that, although I had used the stories as a way to pass time, she had seen them as my way of showing I cared about her and was not angry or disappointed in her. I had helped her in spite of myself.

In other cases, it is just as easy to lose perspective when focusing too much on an individual or group. The following incident exemplifies such a case.

The summer before my senior year in college I worked as a recreational therapist in a mental hospital. Theoretically, I was responsible for about 900 patients, but lack of time and training forced me to concentrate on those who were fairly young, needing activity, and in some contact with reality. Since activities such as hitting a baseball, kicking a soccer ball and running races all help relieve tension and require cooperation, I decided to form some teams. The men had a full sports program, but the women had nothing, so I formed teams for the women, which would give them the opportunity to play regularly. The basis for women to join a team was personal desire, as contrasted with the men's teams, which required special training and selection. The men also competed regularly with teams from other hospitals.

In order to be allowed to play on these teams, the women had to behave on the wards; if they were unruly or disruptive, their attendants would not let them out. As their interest in playing grew the women began to waste less time, and obeyed the necessary rules. They played all positions, each one taking her turn as referee, and some even learning to coach. When the summer was two-thirds over, I thought many of the women were ready to play teams from other hospitals. By participating in sports events with other hospitals, as the men did, patients had the rare privilege of getting away and visiting a new place. I convinced the director of my program that the women had a good team, and should go with the men the next time they played. The only tension of the day came when the director got on the bus and said to me: "If you win, maybe we can make this a regular event." I wanted to win by a score of 100 to 2, so he would be forced to admit that the women were equally capable, and that sports were as valuable an experience for them as for the men.

Some of the women had been inside the hospital for ten years, and had never been allowed off the grounds. They didn't know where or what to look at first; everything interested them. Once they arrived at the other hospital, they exchanged reassuring looks. As guests rather than patients, they were given a lovely meal, a spacious room to change in, and freedom to roam over a large area.

Full of confidence, my team ran out on the field, and the game was off to a good start. They threw themselves whole-heartedly into the game, and at the top of the fifth inning, the score was 4 to 0 in our favor. This suddenly changed as the other team scored three runs. By the eighth inning, the opposing team had scored two more runs, and the score was 4 to 5 in their favor. I called a time out to talk with my team. They were clearly enjoying themselves, and confident that in the next inning they would pull ahead. I was not convinced, and proposed that they send me in as relief pitcher, since their pitcher, a 42-year-old woman, looked tired. Reluctantly, they agreed. Taking her place in the line-up, I hit a long hard drive with two women on base, and we won the game, 6 to 5.

The men, whose game had ended before ours, cheered our victory. Even the other team showed more exuberance than my women. None of them looked directly at each other. Finally one of them told me, "It was nice of you to help, and we know you meant well, but we wanted to do it ourselves."

Being so dependent, they had wanted to be independent at least this one time; it was more important to them to accomplish something by themselves than to win the game. I vividly remember their faces, though the incident occurred more than seventeen years ago; they were full of frustration and disappointment. I had made them pay too high a price for their win; it did not matter to them what the score was, what mattered was that they were trusted to play without supervision. I made another silent promise to myself: not to help people out of difficult situations until they exhausted their own resources, and asked me for help. I felt even worse when the director told me that evening that he could not schedule any more games, since the men had finished their season. My patients would have to wait for the next spring, and another therapist.

Returning to my final year of college, I kept remembering how well the patients responded to activities, despite the frequent warnings that there would be no response at all. I began to question how teachers decided what methods were effective and which activities were appropriate to different situations; my questions seemed to have no answers. The teachers at college were unsatisfactory as models; again, they were in one world, I was in another. I went on to graduate school, but my questions remained unanswered.

When I started my first full-time teaching job, I continued to feel the schism. My supervisor wanted me to follow a 30-year old manual meant for a 15-student class. My class had 50 to 70 students. I was frightened by my lack of preparation, and the large number of students I had to deal with; I was also angry at the limitations of my training. I had to find a lot of answers by myself, quickly. As was the case in other early successful teaching experiences, I helped my students and myself inadvertently.

I had overheard the girls complaining that they never had anything to do after school, so I volunteered to help them start some activities. Other teachers warned me that I would lose half the equipment, and that the boys would break up our games. Their comments worried me, and I told them to my students, who agreed that such things might happen. Although I was ready to cancel the program, the girls then told me that they had solved the problem by inviting their boyfriends to act as referees and bouncers. They assured me that all I had to do was open the equipment cage, be on hand while they played, and make sure all the equipment was locked up when the playing was over. Although this was a Junior High School, many of the girls were taller and heavier than I. Their reassurances to me were both comforting and funny.

True to their word, the boyfriends came and helped. Although we used several hundred dollars' worth of equipment, only one ball was lost in the eight-week session.

An unexpected result of this experience was improved communication between myself and my students. Responsible for the equipment, I depended on the cooperation of the students, and was thus more vulnerable than most teachers. I talked with the students about some of my own difficulties in trying to satisfy my supervisor, the principal and the students. The girls entered into these open conversations, and told me why they hated the gym program, and how they thought it could be improved. Even the boys, many of whom had already dropped out of school, suggested ways to run programs. We arrived at certain compromises: I would not insist on showers; they would take the responsibility of remembering their gym suits. I would take the word of the girls who were menstruating (letting them watch rather than sending them to the nurse), and they would not abuse the privilege. They worked out a tacit honor system, dealing themselves with the girls who were trouble makers. The more we discussed and dealt with problems, the more pleasant school became for everyone. This way of working proved effective in resolving problems that arose for almost all the students.

As teaching became easier, and explaining achieved more than yelling, I began to think of myself as a great teacher, one who had all the answers. These thoughts were confirmed when I was asked to travel to different schools, to act as a resource person for other teachers. I taught sample lessons, giving teachers ideas on different activities, how space could be used, and how children could work independently. Most of the teachers were not receptive to my ideas; they felt threatened, and could not give equal weight to the feelings of their students. I was young and judgemental. I thought most of the teachers should have been doing something else; they either hated their students or used them to make themselves feel powerful. Although there were a few teachers who were responsive, open and imaginative, most of them continued to teach exactly as they had been taught. Very few questioned their methods or assumptions.

Soon after I began traveling to various schools, I had a chance to work in an enrichment program for children in an inner city school. The program's purpose was to help the children feel better about themselves, improve basic skills of reading, and give opportunity to express ideas in plays, writing and crafts. One of the women in this school had the reputation of being a fine teacher, excellent disciplinarian and hard worker. The children spoke of her respectfully, the parents seldom complained, and her students scored relatively high on national tests. That particular year, however, she had seven boys in her class who could not pay attention, were often in trouble, and spent most of their time in the principal's office. When the opportunity for special programs arose, this teacher recommended that the seven boys be excluded, since they would ruin it for the rest of the children. Purely by accident, I overheard her saying this, and offered to take the seven boys myself. She tried to convince me that I was making a mistake, that they were too destructive. Annoyed by her attitude, I countered with my own determination to work successfully with the boys.

Although I did help them, I know now that I could have been much more helpful if my own rebelliousness had not distorted my vision. In my own way, I had become as rigid in judging attitudes and methods as their teacher. My experience with the boys and subsequent students convinced me that one of the goals of good teaching is to have your students learn to function capably and independently.

Since no one would trust the boys to come to me by themselves, I went to their classroom a few minutes before the class was over, and was invited in. Every child who was not writing sat with hands folded, head facing front, books neatly piled, all waiting for the bell to ring. The seven boys were seated in the back of the room, their heads down, busy writing. To my astonishment and embarrassment, the teacher began telling me, in front of the class, why each one of the boys was bad, how difficult it was for them to learn, and that I should change my mind. I interrupted, saying I didn't want to know these things, the boys should have a chance of starting with a clean slate.

She paused and then said, "They can't come to you today, anyway, because they haven't finished their work yet." Feeling defeated, I moved toward the door, but my eyes caught the eyes of one of the boys, who had dared to look up. Stopping, I turned to the teacher and said, "I am supposed to have these boys when school is over. If you intended to detain them, you should have left word with my office. They will have to make up this work some other time, because I haven't come all this way to waste my time." Anger had prompted these words, making me sound more confident than I felt. The teacher silently acquiesced. I asked the boys to follow me, and we left the room, while I wondered what further trouble I had caused them.

I had intended to teach them some tumbling, but it was clear that they were too tense to listen, even though they wanted to. Desperately looking for a way to help them relax I told them to go down to the courtyard and run many times, back and forth, until they were ready to drop. They looked at me as if I were crazy, and then took off. I sat down on the floor to make some charts, wondering if they would come back.

Not only did they return, but after they got over their shock of seeing me on the floor, they proudly reported how many laps each had run. I entered the number of laps on a chart, and suggested that each time, before working, they should run as much as they needed. Although the period was almost over, one of the boys noticed some of the chart headings, which included rolls, jumps, leaps, story-telling and picture making. We spent the rest of the allotted time and an additional half hour exchanging ideas on what to do with our time in the coming weeks. Obviously, it is easier to deal with seven than twenty-seven, but I was immediately struck by the difference between the teacher's description of them, and my own observation of enthusiasm, concentration, skills and discipline.

Our sessions followed a pattern. After being dismissed from their last class, they would run for as long as necessary, and then enter the number of laps and time on a chart. Each boy competed against himself only, in order to improve running speed. The activity for each coming session was decided during the previous one, so each boy knew what equipment to get out and how to set it up.

One day, instead of running, the boys came directly to my room, and sat quietly with their heads down. I asked what was the matter, and one boy, acting as leader, replied "Our class is doing a play and our teacher won't let us be in it 'cause we be too bad." Furious, I wanted to confront the teacher, the principal or the superintendent. I told the boys where I was going, but they were horrified and begged me not to. "Well, if you don't want me to go, what do you want me to do?" They shouted their response: "We want to do our own play and show that dumb teacher!" They expected me to tell them what to do, and were startled when I asked them what they wanted to do a play about. They retorted, "You know we can't make a play. You know we can't read good. You just want us to be dumb." I looked right at them and said, "You are talking about yourselves the way your teacher talked about you. I think you have fine ideas, I know you can make up a play; and, what's more, you will like your own play better than any I might give you. You might even like it so much that you will write down the words and make a book to put in the school library."

Although they were not fully convinced, they were willing to try; the thought of no play at all was worse than making up their own. We spent the rest of our time that day talking about experiences that might work in a play. The boys agreed that their play should be scary, about something "real," and about them, not other people. I suggested they each write a short incident fitting this description, and bring it to class the following week. This provoked a further outburst: "Why do you keep asking us to do things we can't do? You is mean, mean, mean." Finally I convinced them, by promising not to keep what they wrote, or to care about the spelling and grammar. I refused to take no for an answer; my final statement was: "You will do it and I don't want to hear one more word like can't, won't, don't or ain't. That is absolutely, positively enough!" Silently, they filed out of class.

The following Wednesday, during my regular teaching, I was

short-tempered and unable to concentrate. After being yelled at for the third time, unfairly, one of my ninth graders asked, "What's wrong, you've been yelling at us all day!" I started to say "nothing," but thought they deserved a more honest response. I then told them all about the boys, leaving out names and place. My class was fully absorbed, and when I finished, they asked, "Then what happened? Did they write the play?" I told them I would find out later that afternoon.

As they left the class, I could hear their comments: "She should help them more." "Maybe their teacher is right; maybe they are dumb." "I hope they write a good play." "I wish we could write a play." "All teachers are dumb. School is awful. Don't you wish you were sixteen so you could leave?" I wondered if anything I did would make a difference.

On my way to meet the boys, the principal stopped me to ask about the play. My explanation did not convince her; all she could say was, "Those boys are nothing but troublemakers. I don't think they should be given a chance to spoil the work of the rest of the class." Had I really been concerned with the boys' welfare, my tone of voice and answer would have been very different; as it was, however, I just exploded. "You are completely wrong about the boys. They will write such a good play you won't believe it is their work. If you are so worried about them ruining everyone else's, they can do their play just for their parents and friends. They are working very hard, and I am tired of everyone talking about them as monsters." Coldly, she replied "We shall see," and walked back to her office. Suddenly I realized the position in which I had just put myself and the boys. I remembered the women's softball team. I reminded myself that the boys were more important than I was, and thought that next time, I would try to be more diplomatic.

Before they even got into the room, the boys began telling me their ideas. I could not resist a few "I told you so's," which were accepted good-naturedly. It was hardly necessary to read each boy's ideas, since they had been talking about them all week. We put together the outlines of a play, using some of everybody's ideas, and were so absorbed that we lost all track of time. Finally the custodian came and had to throw us out. I glanced at him as we left, the boys full of promises about what they would do before the next session; his smile of approval felt good.

Everything did not go smoothly. It was very difficult for the boys to put their thoughts down on paper, to decide which events to include, and to stage them clearly. Memorizing the lines was not hard because the words were their own. At another point, when no-one could come up with an acceptable ending, the whole experiment looked like it might fail. The boys reverted to their old attitudes: "You tell us how it should end. You the teacher, you supposed to tell us." I refused, saying "If I tell you, it would not be your play. You will have to say it was partly mine, and then everyone will think I did most or all of it; you will be even more mad at me." When I asked them why they could not find an ending, they responded as before, "Cause we dumb." It was much harder for me to refuse to help, but I remembered my softball team, and was quiet.

The next week, they marched in with their script, looking proud and happy. They announced to me: "Lady, would you like to see a play with the greatest ending in the world?"

I sat entranced as they performed their finished script. It was a play about five boys who are punished and have to stay after school. By mistake, they are locked in a closet and have to break out. They get lost, and end up in the basement where they come upon a man with a broken leg, who had given up all hope of being rescued. They discover a way to carry the man out and save him. For their help, they are rewarded with medals, given to them at a dinner in their honor by the mayor. The sixth boy played the injured man, and the seventh boy played both the teacher and the mayor—the latter role was his compensation for having to act the teacher.

The boys did get the chance to perform their play for the rest of the class. There were no comments on why the play was original. The teacher and the principal never talked to me about the play, the playwright/performers, or the book which the boys made from it later. Soon after, however, I was informed that the school did not wish me to return.

Had I been less involved in proving my point, I would have made an effort to enlist the interest and support of the teacher and principal. Now I know that there is no such thing as a teacher who can work effectively with every student. In this instance, the teacher and the principal were teaching as they themselves had been taught. I later realized that part of my job was to help the boys learn how to work with their teacher, within the matrix of the school. I should have communicated to the teacher that the boys were now eager, and ready, to be part of the group.

I have recounted some key personal experiences, and showed how what I learned from these experiences helped me to formulate a way of working that encourages exploration and forgiveness. These experiences taught me that no real learning takes place unless there is mutual trust.

They also have taught me that I myself am always learning, that there are no final answers. Knowing that I have made mistakes in the past, and will in the future, makes me unable to say to students or readers: "This is the *only* way." I am aware that nothing works all of the time, and that teachers are rightly suspect of others who claim to have "the" answer. Often adherence to one method is based on the rejection of all others, and such a single-minded advocacy makes growth impossible.

I hope that the suggestions and activities in the remainder of this book will provide teachers, counselors or parents with the information to structure and implement a more open-ended and flexible way of learning. Nothing is prescriptive. I am presenting a focus, which readers can use as a starting point.

3

groundwork

A teacher's "lesson plans" should regularly include exercises which encourage and reward interesting as well as "right" responses. This is no more than to underscore what has long been obvious to students of "creativity." Namely that creative thinking involves divergent as well as convergent thinking; the formation of concepts as well as the attainment of concepts. In short, invention as well as discovery.

Richard M. Jones
Fantasy and Feeling in Education
New York: Harper & Row, 1968.

Knowing when and how to start

The best time to introduce an arts experience, especially one dealing with feelings, is when the group needs a change. If the group is restless, try stretching. Find ways of relating this experience to other work. If some of the students are having difficulty writing original compositions, stimulate their imaginations by changing the experience. Have them walk barefoot to feel textures, blindfolded to feel dependency, or tied together in pairs so they have to work together. In social studies, encourage the students to create imaginative situations that will help the group develop insights into past or future events.

To make beginning easier, use simple material and ideas. Connect the known to the unknown by starting with a question such as, "What could this chair be besides something to sit on?" Or, "What could you do if you were angry at someone but did not want to show it?" Know why you choose a specific material to work with, use only one or two at a time, and start with those that are accessible and interesting to the group. It is very difficult for beginners to work with highly charged stimuli; it is easier for them to deal with questions rather than statements. Encourage the group to question. Using the phrase, "What would happen if . . . ?" keeps statements suggestive rather than prescriptive. As the group becomes more involved, it will assume responsibility for finding alternatives, and exploring possibilities.

Arranging space

Everyone would like to have a large, sound-proof, wooden-floored room with light and temperature controls, but this is rarely available. It is possible to work in all other kinds of space, however; a small classroom, a gym, a courtyard, a field, a hall or an office. What is necessary at the beginning is privacy.

Furniture can be helpful when you want to work with levels, obstacles or props. Cleared off desk-tops come in handy. Having to work in a difficult space often stimulates the imagination, if students and teacher work together to decide where and how to work. Try to anticipate and remove sharp edges, loose rugs and fragile objects.

Problems getting started

The most difficult problem is always how to get started with a particular group. How you feel about them, how they feel about you, past experiences, present expectations, peer comment and environment are all factors which affect the work. If you are nervous or unsure, the group will sense it and respond accordingly. It is usually best to begin with some relaxation activities. If you are not sure how a large group will respond to a particular activity, work first with a smaller group of five to eight people. Working with honesty on your part helps the group to be honest, just as admitting fear helps others do the same.

Try beginning the work period by rearranging the room. Think of different ways to keep noise levels appropriate; for example, keep the level low by suggesting people avoid waking the sleeping lion.

If you have to work with the total group at once, encourage volunteers, and have the others select alternative activities, one of which might be watching the volunteers. Point out before you start that it is easier to criticize than to work. Select activities that seem neither masculine nor feminine, and avoid terms such as "dance" or "theatre" which might be overwhelming. Perhaps the word "forming" could be substituted for "art."

Even the most successful teacher will have trouble with some students who may be disturbed, self-conscious, or incompatible. If you can work out alternative arrangements for such students, this will improve relations with the rest of the group. Beginners have almost no tolerance for being teased when they are first trying a new activity; stop the exercise if the comments or atmosphere is destructive.

In general, I have found that problems increase with larger groups, longer sessions, and personal insecurity. It often helps if you can respond openly to difficult behaviour. I worked at one time with a group of 22 college students (16 of whom were male), and two of the students continually mocked their own work and the work of others. They soon unnerved me, and encouraged the others to join them as they seemed more and more in control. I searched desperately for ways to reach them. I realized that the source of the problem was their lack of confidence in me and my work, and a scepticism of the value of such work at all. Aware of the problem, I was able to discover an appropriate solution: I invited a teacher they respected to my class as a guest teacher. He participated in the activities, asked and answered relevant questions. In a subtle way he thus reinforced the value of my work, and connected it to his own, as well as pointing out other applications. After that, he would drop in occasionally to ask the class how they were doing or what they were learning. Within a few weeks the class was working with no fear of ridicule, and little discomfort.

Discovering the cause of destructive behavior helps solve the problem. People seldom mock unless they feel threatened or foolish themselves. Signs of discomfort such as shyness, hysterical or nervous laughter, clowning or mocking can result from the discomfort of the teacher, transmitted nonverbally. Open discussion or role-playing might help; it also might be that the group should work with less threatening activities, such as *making machines, follow the leader,* or *making statues.* It also helps to work with class leaders.

Activities that stress energy, feelings or strange ideas may strike certain members of the group as irrelevant. Look for connections with existing activities. One teacher introduced a science unit on the properties of water by having the class physicalize what happens to water at different temperature and pressures. Personally experiencing the change from water to ice increased the students' interest in watching the change in the water itself; it also made it easier to understand.

Changing the focus of the students from themselves to the solution of a problem is an effective way of getting them to work with greater ease. To help illustrate the notion of cooperation based on group, rather than teacher, effort, ask questions such as: "What would we do if our plane crashed on a desert island? How would we get food, shelter, clothing, or make contact with passing ships or planes? What kinds of people are we? How is each affected by the crash? How do we resolve differences and difficulties?" It is very intriguing to think that you can be anything you want to be; you can try on roles as you might try on hats.

Control signals

Once a group is working, it becomes apparent that you can seldom get a group's attention by outshouting them. In the beginning of my first class, I establish a control signal which is nonverbal, easy to see, and decided upon by the group. Past signals have been: one arm raised above the head; peace sign; one foot and arm out to the side; two arms raised with fingers wriggling. Any member of the group can use it whenever necessary. As soon as one person sees it, he/she also does it, until everybody has caught on, the group is quiet, attention focused on the leader. Practice your signal before starting to work to ensure its effectiveness, but do not overuse it; if done too often, it becomes meaningless.

Teacher participation

Teachers often wonder how much they should participate. In general, I think it is better to participate in some manner because this indicates that the teacher feels the activity is worth doing. It also works as a leveling force. From the beginning, it is important to find ways to shift the focus to members of the group, and away from the teacher. This serves to alleviate another problem, copying. Students copy when they cannot think of their own solutions, either out of lack of confidence or laziness. It takes a great deal of time, encouragement and practice to have people develop their own ideas. Copying can be discouraged by asking, "How do you feel about what *you* did?" instead of, "How do you like what I (we) did?" If the teacher structures the problem clearly, the elements of its solution can be arrived at by the students, with no outside help; once they can solve problems for themselves, they will no longer need to copy. The underlying question which the group must ask itself is, therefore, "Is the problem solved? If so, why? If not, why not?" Judgements of good and bad no longer are relevant.

Setting limits

In the development of short pieces, students often find it difficult to find an ending. The presentation seems to go on forever, audiences get restless, and the teacher uncomfortable. A good way to handle this is to give each group a one-minute egg timer. As the group gains experience, substitute a three-minute timer. The group can share whatever it wants, but it only has the time allotted. Knowing in advance how much time it has, the group can select beforehand the most meaningful parts. Sometimes students will choose to share only their unsolved problems. This silent measure of time delegates responsibility for selection where it belongs, on each group.

Encouraging openness

The more a group works together, the better their rapport. Although this is natural and good, it often gives rise to a feeling of exclusiveness, and a hostile attitude to outsiders. In the beginning, unexpected visitors can disorient a group, or make it more self-conscious, but working to meet this challenge is a worthwhile experience.

One solution is to ask all visitors to participate. Another is to train the group to ignore them. Work so that anyone who is present, visitors or parents, feels welcome to join in.

Just as important as the openness between students and outsiders is the openness necessary between students and the teacher. Often if a problem arises, from external or internal sources, I discuss it with my students and together we find a solu-

tion. When I am honest about my own emotions, students are able to express their own. I do not think that working with emotions causes a group to become difficult to handle; more often than not, the group is already out of control.

Repetition of activity

Some teachers feel that doing something once is sufficient. This is usually not the case, however; repetition of an activity allows several things to happen even if it went well the first time. Most importantly, it is necessary to dispel the notion that repetition is synonymous with failure; that the only reason an activity should be repeated is if it was not done correctly. Doing the same activity at a different time and perhaps under different circumstances makes it possible for the group to compare their work and consider growth. Past experience changes the present experience. The first time a new activity is tried, part of the time is used understanding what to do.

When working with a group, things must be repeated because of the complexity of the interaction.

Teachers should be aware, however, that people often ask to repeat an activity to put off further exploration. If the group seems tired, tense, or having a hard time, choose a familiar activity after a new one has been introduced, to help them relax. The teacher who really knows his/her group can make sensitive decisions as to what or when to repeat.

Length of session

It is usually easier to decide whether or not to repeat an activity, than to decide how long it should last. Sometimes a five-minute stretch is enough to relax and revitalize the group; other times, thirty minutes are needed just to get the group ready to work. It is commonly assumed that the younger a group, the shorter the session. My experiences do not bear this out. A group will be able to continue working with concentration and energy as long as their interest remains. The more students can interact and exchange ideas, the longer they can work. If a group is totally involved in its work, and is not being watched by an outside critic, the capacity to work is also extended.

The following is an example from my experience of a group of very young children who were able to concentrate for a long period of time, without becoming restless or bored. This incident also demonstrates that when the context of an emotion is unknown, people respond without preconception; my anger was not interpreted as "anger" but as "sickness," for which my children sought and found a "cure."

I was teaching creative rhythms to a group of fifteen 4-year olds. My sessions were forty minutes long. When the group arrived I usually had music playing, which they could move to at their own pace. Once, right before I left for class, I had a terrible fight with my son. Walking into the classroom, I realized I was still too angry to work. I was very fond of my group, though, and tried to release my pent-up tension from the anger by going through some relaxation exercises. I sat down on the floor, rested my head on my knees, wrapped my arms around my legs, and concentrated on calming my breathing. I became so absorbed that I did not hear the children come in. Noticing that there was no music on, and then seeing me in this withdrawn position, they came over to me and asked with great concern, "Are you sick?" I responded, "Sort of," and kept my head down. Though I could not see them, I heard them discussing what they thought was wrong, and how it could be fixed. Two children came over to me, one on either side, and said, "Don't worry, we called the doctors and they are coming to help you." They stroked my back, pretended to take my pulse, and murmured comforting words.

Soon, several "doctors" arrived. Each examined a different part of me; one checked a foot, another an arm, another my head. When they finished, they drew around me and cradled me, chanting sounds like part of a magic ceremony. I have no idea how long this went on, but I could feel my anger melting away, and my tension ebbing. Finally, they said it was time for me to get up, since I was now able to walk, and they were sure walking was what I needed. They helped me get up, and in a tight group, still supporting me, we all began to walk. Then one child, imitating my voice, suggested we hop. Another soon suggested that we run. Retaining the tight group, but releasing their physical support of me, we went through all the locomotor activities I had shown them. The last activity they prescribed was swirling, which ended when a gleeful voice shouted, "Fall down!" The whole group, myself included, dropped to the floor, laughing.

When I got up, I was astonished to see a dozen or more parents on the edges of the room. Looking at my watch, I saw that we had worked for an hour, in a class totally directed by the children. I had lost all sense of time, as had the children. The parents, seeing how involved we were, did not want to interrupt, so they had waited until we finished. One parent asked her daughter what she had done that day in class, and I heard the child reply, "Our teacher was sick so we had to fix her."

After the children left, I sat alone in the gym, still transfixed by the magic of the experience. Their involvement and concern touched me deeply. Returning to my home, my son greeted me cautiously, expecting renewed anger. Instead, I picked him up and related to him the story of the "cure." My relaxation, and the transformation of the emotion, eased his tension; the memory of the anger was quickly receding.

Such an activity, directed by members of the group, without any help from a leader or teacher, becomes possible when the participants learn to listen to each other and respond accordingly. The period of time can also be extended by changing the pace or energy level. If the group has been very active, do a relaxation exercise. Also use a relaxation exercise to end a period, if an activity has been interrupted in the middle. Follow this with a brief recapitulation of what was accomplished, and where the next session will begin. This allows the class to unwind, and stimulates their thinking about the next class.

Using the unexpected

Many people judge ideas and actions of others as "absurd," using the term pejoratively, and then dismiss the ideas as worthless. Absurdity can be looked at positively, however, and the ability to feel comfortable with it enables you to explore many more

possibilities. In 1900, the idea of putting a man on the moon would have seemed ridiculous. Often, the most exciting work occurs when people who are not bound to the world of causality and objective reality can suggest a great variety of ideas without self-censoring. There is no such thing as an idea which exists in a vacuum; every thought connects in some way, though often subconscious, to the feeling or event that preceded it.

Being silly or spontaneous should be encouraged, not condemned. The teacher who feels comfortable with absurdity has a distinct advantage, and can use seemingly irrelevant responses to help the group discover new things about itself, as well as discover new ways of working.

A teacher who can use whatever happens will also have a security that makes working with people more relaxing and less frightening. Many activities that look simple and predictable on paper often provoke unexpected reactions in practice. An inexperienced teacher, thrown by the unexpected, may decide that affective activities are too difficult. All new experiences should be looked at as unpredictable. If you take it for granted that you will never know exactly how a group will respond, then you will be more open to the actual response, and able to deal freely with whatever happens. This is why a control signal, selected and practiced by the group, is essential.

It is also useful to examine what was expected and what was unexpected, in the outcome of an activity. The unpredicted elements offer valuable insights into work of individuals and the group as a whole, revealing their relationship to each other as well as to the teacher. Often after thinking about these reactions a teacher needs to change the assumptions made about the group, or the structure of the relationships.

An illustration of this is shown by the experience of a young fourth grade teacher who was having trouble with her class. She was in a workshop for teachers, to help improve communication through creating improvisations from props, and activities such as *making machines* and *exploring space*. The day after the workshop ended, the teacher was trying to teach some math concepts to her class, which seemed resistant and restless. She grew more determined, and the tension in the room mounted. One child said under her breath, "This class feels like a broken-down machine that needs to be repaired badly." The teacher, relieved to find an excuse to take a break, recalled the activities of the workshop, and suggested that the class make a machine.

As they were involved in the activity, another child said, "This machine will never work because this part [indicating the teacher] is no good." The children then led her to the back of the room, and continued to work on their machine. She remained there, quietly, for a long time until another child came over and looked at the teacher carefully. In a loud authoritarian voice this child then announced to the class: "I think this part is all right, it just needs some oil. " Several children came over and gave some oil. Slowly, the teacher assumed the rhythm and purpose of the group.

When the machine seemed to be functioning well, the teacher suggested that they return to their seats, and resume the math lesson. The impasse broken down, she was able to explain the math concepts. After that, the machine activity became a class signal. When difficulties in communication occurred, the class would make a machine to release their tension. In retrospect, the teacher realized that her class had found a good way of telling her that she was part of the problem: it allowed feelings to be expressed without hurting anyone.

Creating good working environments

Few people can work vulnerably while everyone else is clowning, hiding behind masks, or working superficially. But unless someone starts to be open, little development can take place. In order to establish interdependency and connection, use activities such as *tangling, group lean* and *group bounce.* If the group is old enough, an activity such as *free falls* allows individuals to express emotion without focusing directly on it. In the beginning, it is easier to do the physical activities than those which stress psychology or emotion. If a person is afraid of doing a free fall, expresses the fear, and then is encouraged by the group until the fall· is experienced, everyone feels a sense of accomplishment. If nothing is expressed, there is nothing to react to.

Physical activities not only help people work more openly; they also help people develop insights about themselves. If a person is told to run to a spot blindfolded, and continually misses, he/she will understand the need to improve kinesthetic sense in order to avoid accidents, and will not blame it on "stupidity." If the teacher introduces activities geared to help particular individuals, this gives the group a chance to be supportive and helpful, a unique experience for many.

Success and failure

Stressing exploration rather than achievement relieves the pressure of finding a perfect ending for each activity. Grades, evaluation and criticism, which focus on results, tend to inhibit people, and keep them from trying new things. There are people, however, who cannot believe work is important unless results are measured in formal ways. It takes some time before members of the group understand that in the arts, everything can be the beginning of something else. There are no endings in the conventional sense; there are only stopping places.

Experiment working with the process, rather than the end result, which allows each moment to be important, since nothing must be censored. Most people walk to get somewhere in a particular time, by a particular route. Few are accustomed to walking without destination or time limit. Try having the group walk without a destination. Some might ask why; to look closely at the environment, to observe textures, objects, people.

Even if you stress exploration and eliminate formal testing, working openly often meets with resistance. Do not give up, though, for that will only confirm the group's fears of being uncreative, and they want to be proven wrong.

To demonstrate how ideas develop, use a simple exercise such as passing a roll of tape around, with each person transforming its shape. If someone gets stuck, literally or metaphorically, other members of the group can offer suggestions until all have been exhausted. Get into the habit of asking, 'What other way?" in order to increase possibilities.

It is also important to establish an atmosphere of sharing rather than competing, from the beginning. Play games where no one is eliminated, and help is given whenever asked for. Because sharing is based on trust and equality, it helps people be more open about ideas and feelings. Competition, particularly in the arts, cuts people off from each other, prevents ideas from being explored, and creates an atmosphere of distrust. The advocates of competition argue that it whets the appetite, giving people the incentive to keep going and to surpass themselves. This has not been my experience. I encourage people to go beyond what they think they can do, but they must serve as their own measure.

Fear of failure, or failure itself, viewed as something to be avoided at all costs, prevents people from experimenting and testing their limits. Creative people admit that they learn more from their failures than their successes, but nobody wants to fail, and the fear of failure is very deep. Some programs go too far in the other direction, and are structured in such a way as to make it impossible for participants to fail. They feel confident and may learn more easily, but this creates a false sense of security which does not prepare them for living.

Feelings about failure are formed by the responses of others.

It is easy to make a child feel terrible by asking, "Why did you fail? Are you stupid?" Instead, ask, "What did you learn from the failure? How will you work the next time?" In this way, the child learns how to use the experience of failing productively. It is necessary to remind people that failing is not a measure of personal worth; to fail in one skill or discipline is not to fail in all. Work in the arts provides chances for experimentation, even knowing that the odds are against successful creations occurring all the time. There are many reasons for failure: some ideas work better than others; some are proposed too soon; others are too far removed from the group's needs and abilities. It helps people to remember that they cannot discover new ideas until they find·the old ones no longer work.

Solving practical problems

Good work is not possible under certain circumstances, such as when the group is tense, enervated, interested in the future rather than the present, or affected by weather. The teacher must be aware of and deal with such conditions. A good way to ease tension is to do relaxation activities. Running, shaking and vibrating exercises relieve lethargy caused by boredom, but not that which is caused by hunger, heat or physical fatigue. Another good way to start is to have the total group create a fantasy based on its mood. For example, if the group meets from five to seven at night, and people are hungry, have everyone bring in a snack for someone else. Have each person describe what they would like to be eating, and pretend to eat it. Or, if students are worried about an exam, have them act out what they will do when it is over.

If a teacher has to teach something that day which cannot be postponed, but the group mood is counter-productive, dealing with the mood makes it possible to do the necessary work later. When there is not enough time to deal with the feelings, often just recognizing and respecting them will suffice.

The teacher should try to be frank about the relationship with the group, what is communicated nonverbally, and how the general attitude makes the teacher feel. When the group understands the important role it plays in determining the quality of the learning environment as well as individual experiences, the group will become more actively helpful.

Sharing and showing work

There is much discussion about whether or not, and when, students should perform. To avoid confusion, I will define the following words as they are used in this book.

Sharing involves the presentation of work to others who are carrying on a similar exploration. (One part of a group shares an activity with the total group.) This is the most informal way of working with an audience. Emphasis lies on encouraging more exploration, and developing new ideas.

Showing involves the presentation of work to others who could be doing a similar activity, but at a different time, space, and in a different group. (One class shows something to another class in the same school.) This is more formal, different classes work differently, and look at presentations differently. Take care to protect those showing their work from criticism from other classes, since another class's evaluative criteria may not be consis-

tent with their own methods. Encourage comments on how to extend the work, but preface all work with a discussion of that group's way of working. It is better to stop a person whose comments are destructive, explaining why, than to allow such comments to continue.

Performing is the most formal way of presenting work to an audience, although its range includes everything from improvisations to totally planned or scripted productions. This last type of presentation is generally outside the purview of this book. If students do perform for an invited audience, take care to protect the performers from pressure and criticism.

When children paint, no one expects to put a frame around the result; but when they work with movement, drama or music, many expect a finished performance. In preparing plays, dances or recitals, it is important to ask: Who will see this work? Why? Should beginners, regardless of age, be encouraged to show their work to people not involved in the creation of it? I think not.

To accomplish a specific goal within a fixed time, it is necessary to sacrifice experimentation with possibilities. In a program whose purpose is to help people externalize their feelings, however, this is too high a price to pay. Beginners should concentrate on themselves and their group, developing skills and confidence. Exposure does not speed up or support such development. If the school play has to be performed, let volunteers work on their own material, and stress the communication of feelings and the development of individual ideas.

In general, material should be shared only with members of the group and those directly related to it (other classes in the same school). The director's or teacher's ego should not determine the major aim of an aesthetic experience.

If the sharing remains casual, self-consciousness is minimal. People under these circumstances can become comfortable when observed. This can happen only if the comments are non-judgemental. Try limiting the type of comments. Suggest that people talk about themselves, not about others; have them share what they see or hear, not whether they think something is good or bad. Instead of saying, "You speak so I can not hear or understand you," the question can be stated: "I have trouble understanding what you say." The first might put the speaker on the defensive; the second avoids the notion of blame. Also suggest that all comments relating to quality be questions rather than statements. People should get used to looking at a work without feeling they have to attack or defend it. Try to preface suggestions with "What would happen if . . ." Those about whom the comments are made should write down helpful suggestions.

When the group can share openly with peers, has confidence, and has developed good rapport, then it can consider showing or even performing for outsiders.

Resolving personality conflicts

Some people use their comments on others' work to score points for themselves, to appear brilliant or perceptive. This problem is eased by limiting comments to questions, having students talk in the first person singular, and avoiding words such as *good*, *bad*, *interesting* and *boring*. If a conflict does arise between two people, role-playing may help. Or, the two could discuss the matter privately. Whatever the solution, the teacher should try to avoid the role of judge. The responsibility of deciding, if the two people are unable to come to the decision themselves, should be shared with the group. With older students, one helpful technique is to make up a new problem, and have the antagonists work it out together. Sometimes isolating the troublemakers allows the rest of the group to work in peace, and shows those fighting how much damage they are doing. Expect people to get along, and to respect differences, and encourage them to live up to these expectations.

Occasionally two students who do not get along reflect a division within the class, and receive support from their respective sides for causing disruption. This is difficult to settle. When antagonistic behavior is displayed, notice spatial relationships. Often there will be a clustering around two individuals. See what happens if you ask the class to freeze, and exchange the apparent leaders, placing each in the center of an alien cluster. This can be used to openly externalize the conflict. A frank discussion, avoiding personal slurs and accusation, also helps.

Sometimes such discussions, or asking for cooperation is not very effective; instead, try activities which demonstrate the need for cooperation, and establish it, such as *tangling*, *two or more partner stretching*, or *working with a partner*. The teacher should keep a diary of difficult incidents; with older groups, the whole class might keep a diary, too. Observations, noted over a continued period of time, will begin to fall into patterns, and underlying attitudes and causes will become clear. Also, by having several people read their version of a specific incident, students will see how observation can be subjective, and will gain insight into the nature of conflict itself. It will then perhaps be possible to evolve a technique for dealing with conflict, in and outside the classroom.

The most difficult conflict of all can be that between a teacher and one or more students. Teachers are either ashamed or unaware that they dislike particular students. If you know what kind of student you generally have trouble with, this helps. Once the source of the conflict is acknowledged, solutions often suggest themselves. For example, one teacher had great trouble working with quiet, passive students. Their docility frustrated and angered the teacher, making him sarcastic and irritable. It was only after several years of teaching that one of his colleagues, who had great respect for his teaching ability, pointed this response out to him. Forced to confront this, the teacher made an increased effort to understand and deal with passive students. Although such work was difficult, it was no longer impossible.

If the students are mature, the teacher could explain the source of difficulty; not as an excuse, but as a way of asking for the students' help. As a last resort, if the conflict is severe and no resolution possible, exchanging students with another teacher is an alternative. This would protect the students.

Although teachers and administrators do not like to admit it, it is true that no teacher works equally well with every student. Nor does every student respond to every teacher. It is necessary to accept this; it could spare many people from pain.

Television

When looking for ideas and source material, many people unconsciously or consciously turn to television material. This influence can be minimized if the teacher offers certain qualifications: for instance, if violence is used to solve conflicts, eliminate violence as a possibility for solution. Other sources—books, pictures, objects, photographs and personal experiences—should be readily available to the students.

Alternatively, the teacher could ask the group to watch a particular show for the express purpose of developing alternatives from the given situation. The program itself would then serve as a point of departure for further exploration.

One group experimented with changing the channels, to study incongruity. This was then translated into a classroom improvisation. A group of students improvised a situation using words, gibberish or silence, as they chose. The rest of the group, watching, could shout "Freeze!" whenever they wanted. Those working would stop, and when the group watching commanded, "Ok, you're on!" they would resume work, but changing characters, situations, and sounds.

One teacher who was fed up with television restricted her students so they could use only personal experiences as source material. Although they found this unfair in the beginning, the students became more and more interested in examining their own lives and ideas. If a teacher can bring in material that is provocative and encourages the class to do the same, the problem of television will be solved.

Accepting the worth of imagination

Some people, even young children, are trained to regard only cognitive work as important. It is the teacher's job to ask questions, the students to answer. It is also taught that there is just one right answer to a question; thus, students feel uncomfortable and lost when presented with several equally valid solutions. It is these students who have difficulty recognizing the value of movement, drama, art or music, and their opinion often influences the rest of the group, causing defensiveness about the importance of creative work.

Students who demand that work be restricted to a narrow intellectual approach are generally rigid, and afraid of change and new challenges, which might reveal their inadequacies. Working with the arts, which involves acting spontaneously with unknowns, is feared because it seems so difficult in its openendedness. When the teacher works without becoming defensive, and believes that the arts have an important place in the total curriculum, this will be reinforced and communicated nonverbally to the students. The attitude of the teacher is the most important factor in convincing students that work in the arts is meaningful and necessary. The teacher who finds ways of con-

necting cognitive and affective experience offers students the richest educational experience possible.

Non-verbal communication

The teacher looks at a student, smiles and says, "I know you didn't mean it; now go back to your math." In spite of the conciliatory words, the student is not convinced. Why? Maybe there was tension in the voice, rigidity in the pat on the shoulder, or resentment in the eyes. The nonverbal communication, transmitted often unconsciously by tone of voice or physical state, undercuts and often contradicts the verbal communication. Although young children are particularly sensitive to such communication, all people are affected by it.

If a teacher is uncomfortable with a particular activity, the class will pick this up, in spite of the ways the teacher might try to hide these feelings. For inexperienced teachers, who are ambivalent in their use and commitment to the arts, it is best to be open, and express such feelings. This will elicit honest responses on the part of the students.

Have the class practice describing what someone does, and how that person seems to feel; this will show the group how most people give mixed signals (words say one thing while gestures and tone reveal another). Students should try to describe internal as well as external realities; this is very difficult to do, however, and failure to do this accurately, for yourself or for others, results in wrong conclusions and faulty judgements. Until people can describe, with some degree of accuracy and honesty, what they perceive in themselves and in others, little exploration can occur. When the effects of gesture, tone of voice and body tensions are understood, the class will be more sensitive to what people are "really" saying, and will be far more helpful to each other.

Exploring dreams

Many teachers are hesitant to ask students to talk about their dreams, because they do not wish to violate privacy or act as therapists. It is possible to examine dreams if the teacher uses the content without interpreting it. I do not try to explain actions or characters within students' dreams; if a person is seriously bothered by them, I suggest he/she talk with parents, counselor or therapist. It is possible to use the images and energy of anger, fear and frustration without knowing their cause. Avoiding psychological interpretation or judgement allows people to work without being embarrassed or feeling exposed.

Dreams provide a rich and exciting source of ideas for work in the arts; they are an especially good source for people who have difficulty inventing stories. Nightmares have provided my classes with thrilling experiences as the students figure out how to re-create falling, being endlessly chased, running through fire, walking on water. I often ask students to write down, anonymously, a favorite dream or nightmare for the class to explore. Sometimes, the class collaborates and creates a group nightmare, combining several fearful events. The group comes to understand the fears of others, and develops new insights, without using the fear itself as the focus.

Working with troubled and/or medicated students

Many children in public schools have been diagnosed as "hyperactive," and are put on drugs under the care of a physician. Some of these children do need special attention, but one of my experiences also proved the contrary.

I was giving a workshop to improve self-concepts of teachers and children, and was asked how to handle a child who had been taken off medication by his father, and who was a terrible problem in the classroom. The child fidgeted, could not concentrate and distrubed the other fourth-graders. The teacher's classroom opened out onto a courtyard, so I suggested that he be allowed to run as much as he wanted every morning before coming into class. The boy was to receive only one direction at a time, and when he could not sit still, he was to be allowed to go outside and run. Several results occurred immediately. The other children became jealous of his running privileges; also, the boy's behavior in the classroom improved so drastically that he soon asked the teacher to give him two directions at once.

In the meantime, the school authorities discovered that the boy was living in a small trailer with an elderly grandmother. She was afraid her grandson would get hurt by nearby traffic, and refused to let him out of the trailer except to go to school. All he could do was watch television, read, and do his homework. By the time he got off the bus at school, after twelve or so hours of confinement, he was like a sprung wire. The school finally convinced the grandmother that the boy needed to go out to play. Within a short time, the boy ceased to be a problem, and the whole class, who had also incorporated running into their daily activities, improved their physical fitness significantly.

If people under medication are sleepy or slow to react, they must not be put in taxing situations. The teacher should know what medication a student is taking, what reactions to expect, which environmental influences (such as the sun) might affect him/her, and what to do should a reaction occur. A teacher should also know when the medication starts to take effect, when it begins to wear off, and how to handle the person between doses.

A teacher should also know if a person is being treated for other kinds of problems. Psychiatric counseling often increases sensitivity to situations. If a person in your group appears troubled and in need of professional help, try to arrange for a professional to work as part of the group. This is preferable to external observation, which usually affects a group adversely. If this is not possible, the local mental health association can offer assistance.

Coordination problems

Although everyone who is poorly coordinated has not had marginal brain damage, many have, often without knowing it. Those with coordination problems need to work slowly, without pressure and with understanding from the rest of the group. Removing the person from the activity is the least desirable way of solving the problem, since it draws more attention to the person's weaknesses, and takes away the chance to practice, which is necessary for improvement. Watch children in particular to see if they have trouble doing simple rhythmic patterns; if they confuse left and right, and if spatial concepts of up, down, back and front, present difficulties. Report such observations to the reading teacher, nurse or guidance counselor so the child can be examined for vision and learning problems caused by neurological dysfunction.

For further information on learning disabilities, the following books are helpful: *Neurological Organization and Reading*, by Carl Delacato (Charles C. Thomas, Springfield, Ill., 1966); the *Journal of Learning Disabilities* (Professional Press Inc., Room 1410, 5 Wabash Avenue, Chicago, Ill., 60602); *Something's Wrong with My Child*, by Charles Mangel (Harcourt, Brace, Jovanovich, N.Y., 1974); and *Learning Disabilities*, by James and Joan McCarthy (Allyn & Bacon, Boston, 1972).

Guessing

Teachers commonly give problems such as, "Act out someone working," or "Act out your favorite animal." Those watching the presentation are asked to guess what the person is doing, or what kind of animal it is. Then, as soon as someone guesses the answer, the person stops. If no one can guess correctly, the group feels frustrated and cheated. Guessing in this manner is a learned, rather than a natural, response. It precludes multiple answers and discourages imaginative speculation. Although guessing might be defensible in an acting program, it is out of place in the classroom.

Instead of asking, "What is the person acting out or doing?" ask, "What *might* the person be doing? What images come to mind when you watch the work being done?"

These new questions make the person asking more aware of certain biases and assumptions which often go unnoticed. This open-ended questioning also leads to examination of why people see what they see, and is an aid in objective description. This in turn encourages the person presenting an idea or action to be adventurous and to experiment with absurdity.

Critical thinking and perceptual awareness

Conventional education, which involves an educator asking a question and a student answering it, is often justified on the grounds that students do not know enough to ask good questions. Learning how to ask good questions, however, can only be developed in an open environment. By asking the group to tell what an image might and might not be, the teacher encourages critical thinking. This process also helps develop an understanding and acceptance of paradoxical behavior. Working in the arts provides problems which have no one or correct answer, especially when based on feeling, so there are few experts, and more possibilities to explore.

To develop good critical techniques, the students must understand how they make a decision. If you know that what you see depends on how and why you look, what you look at, and what you expect to see, then you can understand how different people can see the same thing in different ways. One exercise is to have the class read plays and stories, and decide from whose point of view the story is being told, and how the story would change if the point of view were changed. Or have one group look at an incident (real or staged), and have another group, looking at it from a different vantage point, describe what they saw. Taking close up photographs of ordinary objects provides another kind of perspective. Even without a camera or microscope have the students examine things very closely. Realizing that everything exists in relationship to everything else helps teach tolerance and understanding.

In the beginning, most people judge in absolute terms: good and bad, right and wrong, white and black. The arts permit people to look at something from many points of view, to explore nuances. The ability to develop alternative points of view promotes a more complex view of ideas and behavior. This experience can be applied to the study of language arts and social sciences, where there also exists the possibility of developing alternatives.

Having accepted multiple points of view, it is possible to question freely, without fear of ridicule.

Developing flexible lesson plans
If you have always worked from detailed lesson plans, working more flexibly is difficult. There is no easy way to decrease the initial anxiety. Think of planning as a cafeteria with multiple meal choices. Practice changing from one plan to another quickly, with the help of your group. Start one activity and then invent a new

situation that requires a shift: an important visitor is coming; a storm cuts off all lights and heat; you lose your voice or sight. Ask the group to offer new causes for shifting. One group suggested the floor being covered with molasses; fog filling the room; and the presence of an angry skunk.

You might also try planning only half of the period, and then inventing the second half based on what happened in the first half. Or plan general activities such as painting feelings, and let the feelings of the group at the time determine the activity that will stimulate painting.

Using the moment to determine succeeding events is a skill that the group should develop, to encourage spontaneity. This skill is analogous to a cat's fall: no matter how it is thrown or jumps, the way it lands is always graceful and relaxed. If you and your group are able to work flexibly, you will be more self-assured when you give a lecture demonstration or presentation. One time when I was leading an open class in movement with twelve students, in front of parents, teachers and other students, my mind went blank. I had told them to find various ways to skip, and as I was waiting for them to finish, I could not remember what I had planned to do next. To gain time, I had them repeat the problem over and over until it became difficult to find new variations. Although I saw that they wanted me to change the activity, I could not think of any new ideas. Finally a girl said, "All this skipping is turning my insides into scrambled eggs." This freed me of my mental block; I made an immediate association and gave them a new problem: "Move as if you were eggs being scrambled, cooked, and turning into an omelet." The group responded with great amusement, my brain was no longer paralyzed, and the audience had no idea that anything had gone awry. The group enjoyed helping me out of my predicament, and were happy that they were able to do so.

If real education consists of helping students develop ways of dealing with unknowns, then working flexibly, spontaneously and creatively is a crucial part of the learning experience. By keeping the lesson plans flexible, the teacher can concentrate on group response, and work to create a more relaxed and confident environment.

4

evaluation

Evaluation is best looked at as a form of educational intelligence for the guidance of curriculum instruction . . . Evaluation, to be effective, must at some point be combined with an effort to teach, so that the child's response to a particular process of teaching can be evaluated . . . A curriculum cannot be evaluated without regard to the teacher who is teaching it, and the student who is learning it . . . Curriculum evaluation must, to be effective, contribute to a theory of instruction.

From
Seven Postulates Concerning Evaluation
in
Toward a Theory of Instruction
By Jerome S. Bruner
Cambridge, Mass: Harvard University Press, 1966.

It is generally agreed that quality in learning is harder to evaluate than quantity, and that we tend to measure that which we can quantify. There is little agreement, however, on when and how to evaluate, because evaluation is relative, and depends on who is evaluating whom. In this book evaluation is used to provide a frame of common reference for students, teachers and administrators.

In order to measure something, it is necessary to know exactly what you are measuring, how to accomplish this measurement, and how to determine its accuracy. The activities in this book give form to feeling through the arts, which make them even more difficult to measure. There has been little research in this type of evaluation, which means the teacher will have few recognized skills and standards, and no place to go for help. The word *evaluation* often scares people too, because like *criticism*, it has negative connotations.

It is not enough that the activities described here will make learning more pleasurable and relationships more open. It is also necessary to evolve acceptable methods of evaluating work, so that progress can be measured, and so the value of such art-centered activities can be substantiated. Administrators, parents and even teachers tend to think of work in the arts as an extra. When the budget is cut, arts are the first to go. The importance of math, science and language has been demonstrated; now it is time to establish the unique contribution of the arts to the process of learning in general, and to the individual development of students and teachers.

The program of evaluation that follows is only suggested; students and teachers are urged to develop their own. If careful records are kept showing how the evaluation program is developed, students and teachers will see how much this process encourages the development of critical thinking.

Generally, there are five types of evaluation: I. Student-Self; II. Student-Student; III. Student-Teacher; IV. Teacher-Self; and V. Teacher-Administrator, similar to Teacher-Parent. The method of evaluation suggested here is patterned after the type of questions asked in the activity sections.

Student-self evaluations do not need to be shared with anyone, although the group as a whole might develop the questions. Knowing some common questions helps people deal with similar problems, and answering these questions helps people focus on what they are learning and why. New questions, or re-examination of questions at different stages will, in themselves, provide a measure of growth. The following are examples of the three major types of evaluation.

I. Student-Self Questions

1. Do I participate in posing and exploring problems?
2. Do I hesitate before making suggestions?
3. Do I consider other people's feelings when offering suggestions?
4. Do I feel uncomfortable with the notion of make-believe?
5. Are there people in the group whom I do or do not prefer to work with?

6. Do I know why I feel this way? Do different activities change my preference?
7. Do I censor or judge my work before I do it?
8. What criteria do I use to judge my work?
9. Do I understand what a particular problem involves so I can decide how I feel about it?
10. How do the comments or attitudes of others affect me?
11. How much do I rely on the teacher or leader to form my opinions?
12. Whose opinion matters most to me? Why?
13. How do I feel about myself? How does this influence my feelings about my work?
14. Does working with feelings affect my work in other areas? How?
15. Does working with feelings affect my relationships at school or at home? How?

II. Student-Student Questions

1. Did all members of the group participate fully in the activity?
2. Did the group concentrate on the specific problem to be solved?
3. Could all members participate in ways that felt comfortable to each?
4. Did the improvisation depend more on narration (explaining) than on action (showing and doing)?
5. Was enough rapport established to permit each member

to adjust to unforeseen circumstances? If so, how? If not, why not?

6. Did the ideas used come from all members of the group or just a few?

7. Were people able to listen to each other's ideas, or were they more interested in presenting their own?

8. Could the group communicate to observers what it had set out to?

9. Where did the ideas for the work originate? How might they be developed further?

10. How were differences of opinion resolved? Did the means satisfy most people? How were they determined and used?

11. Did someone have to act as leader, or was the group able to function communally? How was this decided?

12. What was learned from this experience?

13. Did the group enhance the work by using sound, color or texture where appropriate? How did the group decide to use or not to use these?

14. How would the group change the work, given the chance to do it a second time, having learned from the first? Why?

V. Teacher-Administrator or Teacher-Parent Questions
(Each general category deals with a skill necessary for human growth and development)

A. Developing Cooperation and Interdependency

1. Do students feel free to ask for help, and to admit when something is not understood?
2. Is the teacher able to admit when he/she does not know something?
3. Does everyone in the class (including the teacher) share the solving of difficult problems?
4. Can students suggest ideas without feeling hurt if the ideas are not used?
5. When working on group projects, do students feel the need to sign their names, or single out their particular contribution?
6. Is there respect for different levels of competence, so students are able to work openly with others of different ability?

B. Developing Spatial Awareness

1. Are students able to work without feeling they may be bumped into or knocked down?
2. Are students able to stop instantly or shift direction quickly?
3. Do students know how to fall safely regardless of floor type?
4. Are students aware of, and able to use, peripheral vision?
5. Do students have the ability to control direction, intensity, pace and rhythm in movement?
6. Are students aware of their environment so that they feel

safe, and accidents caused by falling over into objects seldom occur?

C. *Developing Sensory Awareness (Kinesthetic, Visual, Auditory, Tactile and Perceptual*
1. Are students gaining increased awareness of vision, hearing, kinesthesia, taste and smell?
2. Are students able to use personal resources (perception of sensory stimuli) to invent multiple solutions to problems?
3. Can students concentrate on one sense by excluding other sensory information?
4. Have the students' abilities to perceive objects, sounds, situations or environments changed since starting arts-centered work? How?
5. Has their awareness of the effect of nonverbal communication affected perception and behavior? How?
6. What effect has increased sensory awareness had on daily living?

D. *Developing Imagination and Access to Creativity*
1. Are solutions to problems offered spontaneously without fear of disapproval?
2. Do students encourage and explore multiple solutions?
3. Are students able to use each other's suggestions as the basis for their work?
4. Are students comfortable with absurdity?
5. Do the following occur frequently: looking for alternatives, exploring multiple possibilities, and feeling comfortable with differences?

6. Can students find alternatives to personal situations or problems?
7. Are students imaginative or creative about solving problems which arise in other areas of learning, such as language, math or social science?

E. Developing Critical Thinking, Selection and Judgement

1. Do the students know why and with what emotion a particular response is formed?
2. Are questions such as "How is it we do or do not know . . ." part of the process of solving problems?
3. Are the students aware of the effects that: seeking approval, conforming to peer norms, growing up in a particular culture and at a particular time, could have on finding solutions?
4. Are students and teachers able to look at their work or have it looked at without defensiveness?
5. Can students change their minds easily if shown a better solution?
6. Are students aware of information used or not used in evaluating decisions?

All of the above questions can be answered with "yes" or "no," but such an answer is insufficient. The understood question is "How do you know?" The answer to this covers the whole gamut, from subjective to objective, from personal to impersonal. The range is narrower in the arts than in sciences, but what is important is to answer without relying totally on personal, judgemental impressions. The following is a partial list of general methods of evaluation

1. Self-report of students in the form of diaries, oral accounts, check lists or taped discussions. At the end of each session, each student should write how he/she felt the work had gone, in what ways it was valuable, what the feelings were after the activity was completed.
2. Report of the teacher, using the same means.
3. Reports of trained observers, not involved in the work.
4. Observation and discussion of video-taped classes.
5. Objective measurements (to be taken before and after some weeks of working): the rate of absenteeism, the number of suggestions to problems posed, and the amount of time to develop evaluative criteria for each problem.

If someone asked me how I know my students are working more openly, I would list the following ways: My students are sitting closer to each other than they used to; their bodies are relaxed and stay relaxed when work is commented on; they listen fully to others' comments, without interrupting or challenging the speaker; eyes remain focused during comments, and do not avoid the person speaking or the other members of the group; after comments, there is no increase in tension, either physically or verbally; and they do not avoid each other leaving the class. I can document these observations from entries in the diaries I keep of each group's work, including individual responses.

Many teachers may feel they have no time to keep such a diary. Once the teacher knows what and how to observe, however, each entry takes less than a minute to record, and can be an invaluable aid. With experience, diagrams and personal shorthand keep writing time at a minimum, while providing an accurate record of the day's activities and the students' responses to them.

Teaching effectiveness can be increased if basic questions, often taken for granted, are not overlooked. One such question is: Do the students seem interested? The answer is *yes*, if: they enter the classroom eagerly, talking with each other, sharing ideas and trying out past activities; if, when working, they can focus on the person talking or leading, and respond with questions and suggestions; and if they can offer examples of related events in the outside world.

The answer to this same question is *no*, if: students watch the clock; if they sit in isolation rather than in clusters; if they use only part of the available space; if they work slowly and reluctantly.

Viewed in this way, evaluation is not threatening, time-consuming, and purposeless. When used correctly, it provides students with the opportunity to develop critical thinking, and teachers with the opportunity to improve rapport and teaching ability. When the criteria are arrived at by teachers and students together, better conditions for learning are established.

5

activities

What is a blind person? The reply could be, "A blind person is a person who cannot see." Alternatively, the reply could be, "Close your eyes and, keeping them closed all the time, try to find your way out of this room." The first answer contains concise and accurate information; the mind is possibly satisfied. But the second answer leads the inquirer to moments of direct experience, transcending mere knowledge, enriching the imagination, possibly touching the heart and soul as well as the mind.

Brian Way
Development Through Drama
London: Longman, 1967.

SECTION I

It is impossible to put the activities into an order which will suit every teacher and every group of students. Each teacher must formulate his/her own work plan, after getting to know the students and the activities. The teacher must also be flexible enough to change the plan, according to circumstances of the moment, such as weather, exams or personal relationships.

It is also impossible to say which activities are most suitable for a particular age group; instead, I have indicated under the heading *Participants and Space* which age groups would find the activity difficult.

The headings of each activity are fairly self-explanatory. *Purpose* deals with the principal aims of the activity, which are suggested, not definitive. Often the aims appear in many activities, such as "to work imaginatively," "to establish trust" and "to work cooperatively," which are basic tenets of the book. It is not necessary to do the activities in sequence; people can choose activities at random, since each activity is complete unto itself. There is a progression from simpler to more complex activities, though, from Section I through Section IV.

Participants and Space gives the optimal conditions for the number of people and the type of space, but these conditions can vary according to what is available. There are certain general rules: young people require more space than older people; the more movement an activity involves, the safer the space should be; the louder the noise level, the more isolated a group should be; and in activities involving direct emotional responses, the group should have more privacy.

Activity describes the event and shows how it can be explored at the moment. I often suggest sharing work with a partner before sharing with the group. This is an important intermediary step. Working on a one-to-one basis improves the student's ability to articulate and to listen; it helps reticent students, and enables all participants to give and receive some feedback.

Suggestions offer possible extensions and developments of the original event, once it has been completed. The group may explore some, all, none, or make up its own. Many times the suggestions are based on an understanding of the activity, and a level of competence which would allow adding complexity.

Questions are for the teachers as well as the students, and are samples of the type of question that participants should ask themselves, though it is better if they can make up their own. Evolving questions based on personal experience and understanding of the work helps develop critical thinking.

Most of the activities in Section I use physical actions to explore time, space, ideas and responses. They provide the students with a specific focus, other than themselves, which helps to reduce self-consciousness. More experienced students can also benefit from these activities, since they serve to aid concentration, create moods, and establish group rapport.

There are few opportunities given to children of the opposite sex to work together without competition, sexual consciousness, or discomfort; these activities provide such an opportunity. Between the ages of 9 and 12, boys prefer to work with boys, and girls with girls, and encounters with people of the opposite sex cause giggling, clowning and sarcastic remarks. Often the teacher feels uncomfortable working with a co-ed group too, and this is communicated non-verbally to the students, adding to their tension and embarrassment. If the teacher is comfortable around close physical contact, however, this too is communicated, and the approval serves as reinforcement. One of the best places to learn how to conduct healthy heterosexual relationships is in school, where relationships can be based on shared interests and activities.

Adults pose a different problem. They have to work through culturally imposed inhibitions, since it is not accepted in our society for adults to touch each other unless angry or sexually involved. Teachers shy away from physical activities out of fear of arousing sexual interest, but students are usually busy working out the activity at hand so that such fears are rarely justifiable. If a difficult situation should occur, the teacher can always change or stop the activity. In the case of such problems, it is helpful to hold an open discussion, limiting talk to description, and avoiding interpretation.

Although learning to touch a person to express concern, compassion or frustration is not something you set out to teach, it will happen naturally as students continue to work openly with these activities. Touching is not the problem, but becomes part of the solution.

It is often difficult when working with these activities to provide connections between them and other disciplines, such as math or science. Students want to know how the expression of feelings relates to finding a solution to $x + y$. All these realms of knowledge and experience are related by and to an overall philosophy of learning: in which the premium is placed on exploration and discovery, and the integration of thinking and feeling.

WARMING UP

Moving with part or all of the body, everyone can: swing, stretch, bob, vibrate, move slowly without accent, move percussively, and collapse. These movements are good preparation for anything from academic tests, to sports, to artistic performance. Warm-ups prepare the body for more vigorous and concentrated activity; they also provide a transition from a previous activity to a new one. Warm-up activities improve communication in a group by allowing people to work together in an easy, relaxed way. When warming up, avoid strain and exertion. Quick jerky movement is bad for cold bodies, especially older ones. When working on hard, cold floors, warm up the feet by doing easy jumps, hops and leaps, in place and in space. For more specific warm-up exercises, consult the bibliography.

Purpose

To prepare the body for more vigorous work
To relieve fatigue and excess tension

To improve communication between members of the group
To improve concentration and focus

Participants and Space

Any number, large open space.

Activity

The warm-ups are divided into two categories: *General Activities*, such as swing and stretch, and *Specific Activities*, for different parts of the body. There is no total exercise that is perfect, and can be done alone. Once the principle is understood, many activities will accomplish the same purpose.

GENERAL ACTIVITIES

1 *Stretching* is the extension of part or all of the body as far as possible without strain. It can be done alone, with a partner or in a group. Work with various levels and use all parts of the body.

2 *Swinging* is a loose, relaxed movement that starts with energy, continues with momentum, and ends with energy. The free-flowing ease of the swing corresponds to the breathing cycle of inhalation (energy), exhalation (momentum). Swing all parts of the body: torso, head, legs and arms.

3 *Bobbing* is a gentle, easy, up-and-down movement, done with any part of the body in any position. To use the feet properly, land first on the toes, then on the ball of the foot, then the heel, and finally, the knees should bend. This is particularly important when jumping on cold or concrete floors.

4   *Striking* is a short, clearly defined movement done with as little tension as possible. The more relaxed you are, the easier this activity is. Striking helps use excess energy, often a problem for young children. Use all parts of the body.

5   *Vibrating* is a shaking movement that resembles shivering. It is hard to do, and harder to sustain, but is very effective in ridding the body of strain and tension. Use various parts of the body as well as the total body.

6   *Collapsing* may be partial or total, but in all cases, start slowly. In partial collapse, a good image is a balloon with the air being let out. To do a total collapse to the floor, keep the body rounded, and land only on padded parts of the body. Avoid falling on knees, elbows, wrists.

The above exercises can be done on various levels, with all or part of the body; with and without sound; with and without partners. Achieve variety by moving quickly, slowly, up, down, circularly, and so on.

SPECIFIC ACTIVITIES

1   *Head*: Circle the head around slowly, keeping the shoulders still, first to one side, then the other. If neck muscles are sore or very tense, bend the body forward at the waist.

2   *Shoulders*: Circle one shoulder, then the other, going around both forward and backward. Work both shoulders at the same time, or sequentially. Keep fingers and wrist relaxed, torso lifted.

3   *Wrists and Arms*: Extend arms out to sides, flex wrists, extend fingers. Move arms around in a circle, forward and backward.

4   *Torso*: With arms relaxed at sides and head in line with body, circle the torso first to one side, then to the other. Work with knees straight, then bent. Extending the arms over the head while circling increases the difficulty of the exercise. Be careful when circling to the back to avoid strain.

5   *Legs*: Keeping the rest of the body as still as possible, do small hops and jumps in place. Remember to touch the heels to the floor each time, bending the knees as feet touch the floor.

Sore Muscles:

Should members of the group complain that their muscles hurt, suggest that they keep working, slowly and carefully. This insures that the muscles will continue to be used, and the soreness will subside more quickly. Warm baths are helpful. Avoid going out into the cold directly following vigorous activity.

In general, the younger the group, the more the need for vigorous activity. Warm-ups could be repeated for a few minutes every hour to avoid the accumulation of energy, that can cause loss of concentration, fatigue and dullness. Older people benefit from activities such as stretching, which improves circulation, relieves fatigue and releases tension. Encourage people to stretch whenever they need, whether sitting, standing, or lying down.

BALLOONS
Purpose
To explore space using a common image

To use an image to stimulate ideas

To develop kinesthetic sense

To increase vocabulary of movement

Participants and Space
Any number, any space in which there is room to move.

Activity
Working individually, explore the sensation of being blown up like a balloon. Move as if all or part of the air has been let out. Work with several partners in this manner. Try making a group balloon; experiment with how the air will be let out, and what effect this will create. Share some of the work with the total group. Those watching might tell what the shapes suggest to them.

Suggestions
Think of releasing the air very quickly, so the balloon goes into a tailspin. Let the air out very slowly, partially and fully.

Based on the feelings which the image and the experience evoked, create an improvisation. Paint a painting showing how it feels to be in a helium-filled balloon. Work with and without sounds.

Questions
How would it feel to be a huge balloon float in a parade, like the Thanksgiving Day Parade in New York City?

How do you feel when part of you is filled with air and part is collapsed?

What other images can you work with besides balloons?
How do you feel when you are part of a group balloon?
What effect does sound have on the experience?

WORKING WITH A PARTNER

Purpose
To work interdependently
To work imaginatively
To work cooperatively
To work with equality

Participants and Space
Partners, any space in which there is room to move.

Activity
With a partner, find an activity that you can do with each other, but not by yourselves. For example, get up with your backs touching, without using hands. Or, play tennis; or get into an argument. When every pair has its activity, share with the total group. Find a new partner to work with, and a new activity. Share and re-group. If you cannot think of a new solution, ask the group for help. Continue until no-one can think of new solutions (which may never happen).

Suggestions
Have people of different height and weight work together, so the little person is not always supported by the big one. Suggest that people not work with the first idea that comes to them, because ideas are not limited. The more ideas the group thinks of and shares, the more ideas each person will get.

Questions
What kinds of activities come to mind most easily?

Do some activities appeal to you more than others? If so, why?
Can you get ideas from watching other people?
What do you do if you and your partner have different ideas?
How do you decide which to use?
How does it feel to work with someone bigger, heavier, smaller or lighter than you?
Can you see how working with a partner lets you do things that you could not do by yourself?
How do you feel working interdependently?

FOLLOW THE LEADER

Purpose
To work cooperatively
To improve kinesthetic sense
To improve peripheral vision
To work imaginatively with movement and sound
To practice leading and following

Participants and Space
Any number, with room to move and see others.
Young children may need help from the leader, and should work in smaller groups.

Activity
One person starts a movement which is copied by the rest of the group. As soon as everyone is doing the same movement, someone starts a new movement. If two or more introduce a new movement at the same time, the group should decide non-verbally which to follow. If both give up the movement, so there is no leader, the group can stop and start over, or a third

person should contribute. Sounds make the work more interesting. If this activity is used as a warm-up, the group should use all parts of the body and all ranges of sound.

Suggestions

If the group includes a very strong leader, he/she should make an effort to follow rather than lead. If a movement is difficult, when everyone is doing it, it can be changed to something easier. Work to achieve variety in sounds, types of movement and levels.

Questions

Do you generally start an activity or follow someone else?

How do you feel if you begin a movement at the same time someone else does?

Do you persist or quickly switch?

How do you achieve variety, and avoid repetition?

What movements are difficult for you?

What movements do you find embarrassing?

WORKING ON AND OFF CENTER

Centering is a term used in ceramics to describe the position of the clay, in the middle of the potter's wheel, ready to be worked. In movement and drama, the term means that the individual or group is internally balanced and ready to work. I prefer "center" to "balance" since the latter implies immobility or stasis. When you move on center, you have stability, control, a clear sense of direction. When you move off center, you are out of control, unable to determine direction, in a state of flux. If you are able to fall

properly, you can work off center in many activities, such as
swirling, if there is also enough safe space to absorb the motion.

Purpose

    To develop a kinesthetic awareness of self in space

    To develop a sense of sharing center

    To learn when one is in or out of control of one's motion

    To become aware of surroundings (people and place)

Participants and Space

    Any number, depending on the size of the room and ability of
    group.

Inexperienced people and younger children need more space.

Activity

Move by yourself on one foot, then on the other. Explore what kinds of movement you can do without wobbling. Focus on a fixed point in space or in your mind. Experiment with levels and space. Work with one or two partners; then with a group of five or six. Try working off center as an individual, but on center as a group.

Suggestions

Start slowly; working quickly is more difficult. Try to develop and work with an inner sense of focus. Experiment with your eyes open and shut, with and without sounds, with smooth and jerky movements.

Questions

How do you keep centered with your eyes closed? Why is it so much harder?

How do you feel sharing center in a group or with a partner? Is there a difference?

How can you find your center when working off center?

SWIRLING ON AND OFF CENTER

Purpose

To explore how to control one's body in space

To develop kinesthetic sense

To use space consciously and deliberately

Participants and Space

Any number, large open space.

Activity

One at a time, swirl around the room, letting your arms come up as the result of the force of the swing. Try swirling on center, which will result in controlled, even motion; and off center, resulting in erratic, uncontrolled motion.

Suggestions

This is an important activity, because it demonstrates self-control of the body in space. Accident-prone people often have no idea what their bodies are doing, how they occupy space, and therefore are constantly bumping into or falling over objects. Add sound to the swirl. Try swirling with several people at a time. Switch off and on center, with eyes open and closed. Use various levels.

Questions

Can you tell when you are off or on center?

How do you feel when swirling?

Are your feelings different if you are off or on center?

What does swirling make you feel like, or think of?

How do you feel swirling with eyes closed, with others swirling at the same time? When could this be dangerous?

Can you tell if others are working off or on center?

If off center, how do you get on center?

Can you paint the sensation of being on and off center?

Could you create a mobile with these feelings?

Could you swirl, make contact with someone, and then swirl away? What control do you need?

MELTING SNOW, QUICK FREEZE

Purpose

To use tension or relaxation, as desired

To work imaginatively

To respond to images

To improve kinesthetic sense

Participants and Space

Any number, any space.

Activity

Fashion your own snow statue using fluid, relaxed movements. On signal (prearranged sound or motion), each statue should freeze. Again on signal, each statue should begin to melt. One way to begin is to decide where the source of heat is. On the third signal, the statues should begin to freeze again, but taking several seconds. The process can be repeated as many times as desired. Even when the statues are on the floor, totally melted, these shapes can freeze, melt and re-freeze.

Suggestions

If one or more statues begins to melt in another person's space, use this to create a two person snow statue. These people could melt away from each other, remain together, or absorb a third, a fourth, and so on, until the whole group is forming one statue.

Create a real feeling of melting and freezing by working slowly and with detail. Experiment with slow and fast thaws.

Questions

How do you feel when you are melting? Do you feel differently when you are freezing?

Do you sense a temperature change?

How does working as a group statue differ from working by yourself?

Are your perceptions of your body in space accurate? How do you know?

What stories can you invent based on this activity?

Do you prefer working with tension or relaxation? Do you find one more difficult? Does one tire you out faster? Why?

THROWING AND CATCHING

Purpose

To work from kinesthetic cues

To work cooperatively

To respond with realistic action to imagined situations

Participants and Space

Partners or small groups, space for everyone to move.

Activity

Throw an object, such as a ball, to your partner. He/she catches it. Then the partner initiates the action, throwing the ball again, but changing it so the ball (or any object) assumes a different size and weight.

Suggestions

Throw the object in different directions; to one side, over the head, in front, to the feet. Throw it in a way which expresses an emotional or physical state: shyly, aggressively, angrily, seductively, hurriedly, and so on.

Questions

How do you non-verbally distinguish between a knife, a ball, a box and a balloon?

How do you indicate change of weight, direction or shape so your partner will understand?

How can you non-verbally express your feeling about the object or how it is being thrown?

MAKING MACHINES

Purpose

To physicalize inanimate objects

To work cooperatively

To work imaginatively

To explore sound and rhythm

To improve spatial awareness

Participants and Space

Any number, with space in which everybody can move.

Activity

Have each group decide on a real machine. Have each member of the group become part of the machine, making appropriate sounds and movements. When ready, share all work. Make no attempt to guess what the machine is; instead, respond to the images evoked.

Suggestions

Create machines that make something, such as a doughnut machine or a toaster. Also create imaginary machines, some that do, and some that do not, make something. Give the imaginary machines names. If the group has trouble with imaginary machines, start with one person making a sound and motion. Each person in turn then adds a sound and a motion until the whole group is involved. Make the machine move across the floor. Have the machine break down in order to explore ways of fixing it. Use various intensities of pace, tension and sound. Try having each person work on a different level.

Questions

What kinds of machines are easy, or hard, to do? Why?

How does the experience differ when more or less people are involved?

How can the machine serve as the basis for an improvisation?

How can making machines reflect your feelings about people or situations?

What kind of a machine does it feel good to make?

What kind of machine makes you feel anxious?

MAKING MONSTERS

Purpose

To work imaginatively

To respond to fantasy

To create a common fantasy from individual fantasies

To work cooperatively

Participants and Space

Any number, large open space.

Activity

Create a monster, determining where it lives, what it eats, how it relates to other creatures, how it dies. Use simple props or materials, such as cardboard tubing, old wire, colored paper. When each person's monster is ready, share them. Perhaps separate monsters would like to interact or combine to form a group monster. Encourage the group to work with as much detail as possible, so there is diversity and complexity.

Suggestions

Pose problems to each other, such as: How would this monster differ if it lived at the bottom of a lake, on top of a high mountain, in the midst of a rain forest or in a desert? How would your monster be affected by similar monsters or different monsters? Could it live alone? Consider how cold, heat, rain, snow and ice might affect it. Does it relate to humans, can it respond to machines, is it from outer space? The more questions the group asks, the more varied and imaginative the responses.

Questions

How would your monster react to being in school, living in your home, meeting your family, going on vacation?

How was your monster born?

How does it die?

What pleases it? What angers or frustrates it?

What might cause your monster to be sad and cry?

GROUP ANIMALS

Purpose

To work cooperatively and imaginatively

To be aware of how parts form a whole

To create as a group using individuals' ideas

To respond to stimulation as a group

Participants and Space

Small groups with space to move; high ceilings are good.

Activity

Begin with the image of a real animal, such as an elephant. Using groups of 5 or 6, create one such animal, using appropriate sounds, movements. Have two animals meet and explore possible ways of interacting. When finished, share work, re-group, and try other animals. Make the animals as detailed as possible.

Suggestions

Create unreal animals, developing specific sounds, habits, likes and dislikes. Have two or more of these unreal animals interact, using non-verbal sounds; try to find out as much as possible about each animal. Pre-arrange space to represent water, mountains, trees, to give common geographical starting points. When ready, share work, and let the spectators ask questions about the animals. Good questions can help create a story, which later can be written down, moved or acted out. Those watching might paint an environment for others' animals. Or, compose sound and music scores to accompany scenes.

Questions

How do you decide who will be what?

How do you feel as part of an animal, rather than the whole?

Do you like to share the decision of how to respond?

What are the advantages to working as a group animal, rather than individually?

What are the disadvantages? Which do you prefer? Why?

What do you do when most of the people in your animal feel like responding one way, and you another?

Does your group work with or without a leader?

How is the decision made? How do you feel about this?

GROUP BOUNCE

Purpose

To relieve tension

To warm up the body

To establish good group feeling

To laugh (if it occurs naturally)

Participants and Space

Any number, any size space.

On a concrete floor, work slowly and carefully. Remove shoes. Remember to bend your knees as you land to prevent hurting yourself.

Activity

Widely spaced, start shaking some part of your body as easily and with as little tension as possible. As the shaking continues, move or bounce toward other people. As you touch another person, establish a common rhythm. Pairs touch, making groups of four with a common rhythm, continuing until the whole group is bouncing together in unison.

Suggestions

People can start with individual sounds as well as rhythm, establishing a common sound as they merge. Talking while bouncing helps insure even breathing, which lets people work longer without losing their breath. Young children may get very silly when they first try this; keep each group to 5 children or less, and add more later. This is a good way to warm up a group which is physically cold.

Questions

Do you prefer to be on the outside or inside of the group? Does this vary?

Do you ever feel you will be trampled on? If so, what do you do about this?

How do you get a common rhythm? Do you give up your own, do you persist, or do you use a little of both?

What circumstances would make you enjoy this more or less?

BOARDS AND SPAGHETTI

Purpose

To experience and explore levels of tension

To work with confidence with partners

To work cooperatively

To develop trust

Participants and Space

Groups of three (similar size and weight is helpful), with space in which to move.

Activity

Boards Two people face each other (while the third stands in the middle facing one of them) with arms bent at elbow, and palms facing the center person. Standing as rigid as possible, the third person then falls, and is caught by each of the other two. Those catching stand with sides of body facing the faller, arms bent, with feet apart. The rigid third person rocks back and forth, caught on either side by the other two. When all three are confident, the faller can close eyes, and the catchers can increase their distance from the faller. Each person should have a turn in the center.

Spaghetti The person in the center goes totally limp; the two others try to pick all or part of the limp body off the floor, without straining themselves.

Suggestions

If the person falling is afraid, the catchers should start out very close, and move farther away gradually, as confidence is gained.

When lifting a limp person, be careful not to strain. Work with more people if the faller is very heavy.

Questions

How do you feel when you are the board?
How does working with eyes closed change the experience?

How do you come to trust people with whom you work?

Can you tell without looking whether your body is limp or rigid?

Are your feelings toward the people you have worked with different after this activity?

USING GIBBERISH

Purpose

To explore unfamiliar sounds

To release tension

To explore the effect of dynamics in communication

To explore communication without common language

Participants and Space

Any number of partners, any space in which there is room to move.

Activity

Work with a partner, and tell the person how you feel about something, without an understandable language. Develop a conversation with your partner responding in gibberish. Share something about which you feel strongly.

Suggestions

Have people who are angry at each other use gibberish to talk to each other. Explore how gibberish insures privacy, and protects the speaker; set up situations such as telling someone you love them, scolding a child, being yelled at by a superior. Share work with the group, exploring how much communication depends upon inflection, dynamics, gesture, and other non-verbal factors.

Questions

How do you feel using gibberish?

How much can you understand when someone speaks to you in it?

What is easily communicated; what is more difficult?

How would you communicate in a country where no-one spoke your language? Have you or someone you know ever been in this situation? How did it make you feel?

Can you use gibberish to express feelings you are unable to express in your regular language? What feelings are these and when do they occur?

How could you use gibberish in role-playing?

How can gibberish be used when the group is tense or blocked?

MOLDING STATUES

Purpose

To develop kinesthetic sense

To develop spatial awareness

To work imaginatively

To work cooperatively

Participants and Space

Partners, any size group with room in which to move.

Activity

One person is the "clay" and starts in a neutral position, such as standing or squatting. The other person, who is the sculptor, molds the "clay" into any shape, using sounds and movement, but no words and no direct physical contact. When the statue is finished, and the position remembered, reverse roles. When the second statue has been finished, both resume their position and interact with each other, using the total body, non-verbally. (Greet each other, play a game, dance, fight.)

Suggestions

If neither partner can think of an interaction, have the group look at the statues and offer possibilities. Keep the original positions but alter the spatial relationship, such as back to back, side or diagonal. Change the intensity of movement. Add sounds or gibberish. Have the sculptor "breathe" life into the statue with various degrees of energy.

Questions

How do you feel if your partner does not respond as you intend? How does this affect your response when it is your partner's turn to mold you?

What do you look at to decide how you will interact?

How do you signal your partner so your intentions will be understood?

Can you continue to interact until you both feel you have come to an end?

How do you know when you are ready to stop?

MIRRORS

Purpose

To concentrate on precise movement response

To improve kinesthetic sense

To improve spatial awareness

To respond accurately and follow an external movement direction

To improve peripheral vision

Participants and Space

Partners, even-numbered groups (4, 6 or 8); large space.

Activity

Face your partner. One is the mirror, the other is the initiator of the movement. If you are the mirror, imitate your partner's movement as exactly as possible. Switch roles, so both can be mirror and initiator.

Do the activity in groups of two, three or four. Mirror both the individual and the group action. Each person copies the person opposite.

Distort the mirrors, as in a fun house of a carnival. The person who is the mirror chooses the type of distortion (making the movement small, big, wide, narrow).

Mirrors can also have delayed action, so there is a perceptible pause between the movement and the reflection of it.

Suggestions

It is best to start slowly, with simple movements, such as an isolated arm, hand or leg. In group mirror, remember who your partner is as well as what the total group is doing. This is very difficult, and requires more space. Add sounds. Explore emotional and physical levels, and dynamic variety.

Questions

How do you feel if your partner goes too fast or makes very complicated movements?

What do you do when it is your turn to initiate movement?

How do you feel doing a group mirror?

How do you feel when your movement is distorted? Do you like to distort your partner's movement?

FALLS AND FALLING

Purpose

To feel safe when falling

To learn how to fall in many ways

To understand how falling surface affects the fall

To experiment with the use of falls in improvisation

To develop courage and confidence

Participants and Space

Any number, depending on space (preferably large) and number of mats. If no mats are available, have people wear padded clothing.

Young children get excited with this activity; work with them slowly and in small numbers. Older people should warm up first, work slowly and for shorter periods of time.

In general, the person falling should present a rounded, relaxed surface to the floor or ground, and should continue to move after impact to reduce the shock. The motion absorbs the shock, and will reduce chance of injury. Do not use sharp body edges, such as elbows, knees or wrists, to break the fall. Reduce tension in learning how to fall by working slowly. Let each person set his/her own pace.

Activity

Starting from a crouched position, roll back and forth keeping the back rounded, the arms relaxed, head in line with the body but not rigid. Gradually increase the height of the starting position until you are standing, rolling down and then up without using hands. Repeat to each side, careful to avoid knees, hip bones, or shoulder bones.

As confidence develops, fall from a jump. Then fall from a run and a jump. Consult a good book on tumbling (see bibliography at end of chapter) for more detailed instructions about shoulder rolls, front face falls, and other specialized falls. The above skill is included for reasons of safety.

Suggestions

Try falling on different kinds of surfaces. The harder the surface, the more slowly you must work. Incorporate falls into improvisations. Paint the way falling makes you feel. Develop many different ways to fall. Fall knowing you have to get up quickly, because someone is right behind you. Add sounds. Try falling with a partner.

Questions

How you do feel when you fall? Does practicing change your feelings?

Have you ever had a memorable experience with a fall? Could you share this with a group and re-enact it?

What does it take to learn falling so well that, when you fall by accident, you fall correctly?

From what height can you safely fall?

FAST STARTS AND SUDDEN STOPS
Purpose

To develop kinesthetic sense

To develop spatial awareness

To develop inner focus

To develop confidence in controlling direction

Participants and Space

Any number, but begin with one person at a time; space in which to run.

Activity

Establish a point at one end of the room on the floor (a circle or a person at a point can act as the marker). Run as fast as you can, stopping just before you reach the marker. Try this forward, backward (with a person acting as catcher), with eyes open and closed. Work with and without sounds.

Suggestions

When working backward or with eyes closed, have the rest of the group stand around the sides of the room, to serve as buffers if the person heads in the wrong direction. To vary this, have the group form a large circle. The person in the middle then runs to the sound which someone in the surrounding circle is making, movement relating to the type of sound. A low, slow sound would call for a corresponding type of movement; a high, fast sound might mean running on tip-toe. The person moving toward the sound tries to stop just before reaching the source. Give each person a turn in the center.

Questions

How do you feel running with eyes open, compared to running with eyes closed?

Which is easier, running forward or backward? Why?

How does it feel when you are the person in the center of the circle?

Does practice change your feelings about this activity?

TANGLING

Purpose

To explore shapes kinesthetically

To work cooperatively

To recognize feelings evoked from physical positions

To work with care for others

To explore movement possibilities in strange positions

Participants and Space

One person or any number (the higher the number, the more difficult); any space in which to move.

Older people become self-conscious in small groups of 2 to 4.

Activity

When working by yourself, twist the body into a peculiar or awkward shape. When working in groups of two or more, tangle everybody into as complicated a shape as possible, using every part of the body. When no more tangling is possible, smoothly reverse the movement until you return to the original position.

Suggestions

If the group works too quickly, play some slow music. First work individually, then with partners, then include the whole group. See how high the group can reach; how low, how far out it can extend, how much it can contract. See how many eyes each person can make contact with at once; how many elbows or knees can touch? Have the group move as if being chased, and chasing; as if depressed, elated, frustrated, angry.

Questions

Can you move as if angry when you are not angry?

How do you feel when tangled?

Do you trust your partners not to bend your limbs beyond their natural stopping point?

How does moving like this make you feel? Is this feeling always the same?

ADD A MOVEMENT, SOUND OR SHAPE

Purpose

To develop kinesthetic awareness

To improve memory

To develop a sense of group cooperation

To explore variety of movement, sound and shape

Participants and Space

Small groups work simultaneously; space in which to move.

Activity

Each small group forms a circle. One member starts a movement. The next person picks up the first movement and then adds one. All the remaining members do the movements of those preceding, adding one. If a person is unable to remember the sequence, the group can help. Note how long the group can remember it. Do the same activity with sounds, shapes, or any combination. Be careful that each movement is repeated exactly.

Suggestions

Make sure that each person has a chance to remember the sequence without being pressured by the group. If one person always has difficulty remembering, let that person start or be near the beginning.

Questions

Which is harder to remember: movement or sound?

What cues do you use as memory aids?

Does the activity get easier when you repeat it? Why or why not?

Do you like having the group help you if you are stuck?

What do you use to vary movement, sound and shape so you do not repeat yourself?

EXPLORING STRANGE POSITIONS

Purpose

To develop kinesthetic sense

To improve balance

To explore the feelings evoked by moving in strange positions

To work imaginatively

Participants and Space

Any number, fairly large space.

Activity

Assume the most strange position you can. Explore what movements are possible in this position. When each person has done this, share results with the total group. (If the group is very large, divide into 2 or 3 smaller groups.) While watching each person, have the group be conscious of how the work affects it. The emphasis should be on exploring the most extreme possibilities, rather than worrying about realism. Use sounds, including gibberish.

Suggestions

Work with two, then three other people at the same time. Explore additional possiblities of these combinations. When watching the work of others, have the group suggest modifications or variations (such as, how the creation would move if hungry, tired, or afraid of a larger predator).

Questions

What does it require to work in strange positions?

How does working this way make you feel?

How does working with one or two other people change your feelings?

How does keeping an action but changing the sound affect your work?

What would it be like to go through a normal day in a peculiar position?

What do you see or hear in another person's work that tells you what the creation might be, do or think?

How can you use the ideas of others to stimulate your own ideas?

LEAPS INTO SMALL SPACES

Purpose

To learn to move safely in fast moving groups of people

To improve spatial perception and develop courage

To participate in a safe activity that looks dangerous

To work cooperatively

To learn to adjust to quickly changing spaces

Participants and Space

Any number, large space such as a gym or open field.

Young children will have trouble with this, and should work very slowly and carefully.

Activity

Start this activity working with 2 and 2, then 3 and 3, 4 and 4, and so on. Build up speed slowly. Add sound only when the group has good control.

Two people are at one end of the space, the other two opposite them at the other end of the space. The pairs should run and leap so that all finish in close proximity, passing right shoulders. When each person is sure where he/she will finish, repeat the activity with each person touching another coming down from the leap.

Add other people and increase the speed and the volume of sound, but slowly. Finally, the whole group should work together. It is spectacular to watch this activity from the side, where the groups land. It looks as if people will crash into each other, but this should not happen.

Develop a group improvisation, with this activity as beginning or end.

Suggestions

This is good to do when the group needs to release tension. Try to work in a space set apart, so the noise will not disturb others. This activity leaves people exhilarated. Encourage people to work with exuberance as long as they are aware of their space. Make sure people remember to pass right shoulders.

Questions

How do you feel charging into a space that appears to be filled with people?

Does this activity scare you?

How do you develop courage doing something frightening?

Do you accept your fear as a limitation or as something to be overcome?

How does pace affect spatial perception?

How does varying numbers of people affect spatial perception?

Can you shift quickly if a space you thought empty is not?

If this is difficult, how can you improve your skills?

Where might you use this skill in daily living?

BODY-PART CONVERSATIONS

Purpose

To explore non-verbal communication with parts of the body

To explore absurdity

To increase the expressiveness of the body

Participants and Space

Any number, any space.

Activity

Have a non-verbal conversation using elbows, knees, shoulders, or any other part of the body, to talk to someone else's elbows, knees and so on. Talk in various positions with various people. Try talking to yourself: your elbow to your knee, for instance.

Suggestions

This activity usually results in much hilarity. Use it to relieve tension or after activities demanding intense concentration. Explore the serious as well as the comic. Invest different parts of the body with emotional qualities: angry elbows, sad shoulders, repentant knees. Work without using the eyes and mouth to indicate feelings. Try covering the head with a paper bag with eyeholes, so your eyes can be used for vision but not expression. Share work with the total group.

Questions

How do you feel talking with strange parts of the body?

In daily living, why do you choose certain parts of the body to gesture with?

Do people all over the world use the same body parts for gestures? How do you know?

How much of what you do is culturally determined? How much of your non-verbal communication is learned from family, peer group, schooling?

Are some parts of the body more effective than others in communicating? Why? When might this not be true?

What effects do distance, level and environment have on gesture and its use in non-verbal communication?

MOVING IN RESPONSE TO GROUP DIRECTIONS

Purpose

To explore possibilities of movement

To develop balance, coordination, flexibility and strength

To explore various movements through size, direction, tension level, pace and dynamics

To develop self-confidence with others watching

Participants and Space

Small groups in a space large enough to move freely.

Activity

Groups of 4 or 5 should form a circle, and have one person stand in the center. Each member of the group then calls out a direction such as, "Move your right arm in a circle around your head." Each person modifies how the part of the body is to be moved until the group can not think of new ways. Then have a new person step into the middle, and the group should explore a new part. When finished, discuss the work within the group; follow with a total group discussion.

Suggestions

After some experience, this activity will become too easy. Then, instead of starting with individual body parts, each person directs the one in the middle with an overall type of movement, such as: "You are old and lame, and you have to lift a heavy bucket up a steep hill." The next person might add: "You must hurry, in order to get home for dinner." The one after might add: "You are angry because you feel your grandson should have offered to do it for you." If it becomes necessary to add characters, members of the immediate group can join in the action. Work specifically, adding one element at a time, so that each new element can be explored and responded to by doer and watchers.

Questions

How do you feel taking directions from the group?

If you feel the group gives you too difficult an activity, what do you do?

What directions are difficult to follow? Why?

Which are easy to follow? Why?

Do you like this way of working? Why?

How do you feel working in the center with everyone watching you?

If you feel the group is not interested in giving you exciting things to try, what do you do?

WORKING WITH OBSTACLES (I)

Purpose

To develop kinesthetic awareness

To sharpen response to auditory stimuli

To work cooperatively

To experience working without vision

To trust perception of self and group

Participants and Space

Any number, any size space. The absence of objects makes the work easier.

Activity

Divide the group in half. One group should close their eyes or leave the room. The second group should arrange themselves as obstacles which the first group will have to go under, around and through. Use as many levels and shapes as possible. If the group is small, have one-third go through and two-thirds be obstacles. When the obstacles are set and the first group is going through, have a sighted person set them going in the right direction. Sighted people should also warn those who can not see about the presence of chairs, desks, or other objects. When all have gone through the obstacles in the first group, have the groups reverse roles.

Suggestions

If the group gets too excited, play soft music in the background. Each person-obstacle can make a specific sound, and those going through the course should hear a set number of different sounds before they finish. Sounds can indicate whether the obstacles are high or low, should be moved around, through, over or under. People can hold on to each other, or go through separately.

Questions

How does being without vision alter your perceptions?

How do you feel moving through obstacles without knowing where you are going?

What changes when you rely on someone else to keep you safe?

Try painting or sculpting your feelings about this experience.

Could you write a short story based on these feelings?

NEW GAMES FROM OLD

Purpose

To work imaginatively, creating something new from something old

To understand a central concept

To work cooperatively

Participants and Space

Small groups of 5 or 6 with room in which to move.

Activity

Have each group make up a game that they can play immediately. If you can not think of an original game, use a familiar one and change it slightly. Share games with total group.

Moving clockwise, have each group take the game of the group that preceded it, and decide what the central concept of the game is. Keeping the concept, vary the game.

For example: if the game consists of one person starting a motion, and the next one adding one, the concept is adding to what has happened. Vary the game by working at a blackboard, with string, or pencil and paper, having people add a line instead of a movement.

When the new games have been worked out, share them with the total group, explaining what the central concept was, and how it was altered. If time and interest permit, change games until each group has played all games.

Suggestions

When each group has had a chance, ask the whole group to make suggestions. Play out several variations, and discuss which work well, which do not, and why. Avoid games that eliminate people or put undue pressure on individuals.*

Questions

How do you decide what the central concept is?

How else can the notion of taking a central concept and changing it be used?

What are some ways to vary games without changing them totally?

What does it take to change something rather than vary it?

What kinds of games do you like, or not like, to play? Why?

Can you think of ways to make games non-competitive?

How do you feel about competition?

CIRCLE RHYTHM

Purpose

To improve concentration

To become aware of nuance in rhythm

To work comfortably with syncopation

To explore rhythmic movement and sound

Participants and Space

Groups in a circle; space for each circle.

Activity

Standing in a circle, one member of the group claps a rhythm which the whole group repeats. Each member in turn claps out

---

*If the game situation is fun, and people (especially children) have trouble with an activity, particularly one involving coordination, it may be that they have some learning disability. Try to give them a chance to participate in a less stressful way.

a rhythm. As you gain in experience, make the rhythm with other parts of the body. Gradually add sounds. Divide the group in half. Have one new group repeat the rhythm exactly, while the other syncopates it, providing a more complex response. Finally, add body movement, so rhythm, sound and movement are all involved.

Suggestions

Start with *simple* rhythms, sounds, and movements. Work with a tape recorder, so the group can hear how accurate their repetition is. Use a metronome, to see if the group tends to get faster or slower. After some experience, work with complex metres such as 5 or 7 rather than 3 and 4.

Questions

Do different rhythms have different effects on you?

Can changing rhythms change your feelings?

Does a rhythm change if it is played loudly or softly?

If someone starts a fast, rhythmic beat, when you are feeling low, do you find your feelings change?

Does the quality of the sound affect feelings?

Is there a difference in the effect of a bass drum and a triangle?

Can you paint rhythms? Try painting while listening to some African drumming. Then to a piece by Debussy. What are the differences?

Can you remember how the sound affected your work?

CIRCLE PASSING

Purpose

To improve kinesthetic sense

To work cooperatively and supportively

Participants and Space

At least 8 or 9 in a group, with space between groups.

If the average age is under 12, leaders should use their judgement about attempting this activity.

Activity

Each group forms a circle. One person stands in the middle with arms folded; the rest sit on the floor with their feet up against the center person's ankles, to keep him/her in place. If the person is heavy, have 3 or 4 back-up people stand behind those sitting, to provide extra support. The center person begins by leaning toward someone sitting. The person sitting should catch the center person, and pass him/her to someone else (next to, or across, depending on the momentum). Tell the person in the middle if the body starts to bend; it should be extended, but not rigid. Pass the person slowly or quickly, quietly or with sounds, depending on experience. Each person should have a chance to be passed.

Suggestions

If several groups are working at once, start with the smaller people, and then combine to pass the heavier or taller ones. Some people may be afraid that they will be dropped or hurt; in their case, have the group be very gentle, and make no noise except words indicating body position. Work slowly when passing a larger person until confidence is gained.

Questions

How do you know whether your body is bent or extended?

Which is more difficult to catch: a bent or extended body?

Which seems heavier?

How do you feel when being passed quietly? Noisily?

What is the difference being passed with your eyes open or closed?

If you find this activity frightening, how do you overcome your fear in order to do it?

GETTING TO KNOW PEOPLE WITHOUT ASKING QUESTIONS

Purpose

To learn to listen

To make someone feel comfortable

To introduce a stranger to the group

Participants and Space

Partners without a group of any size; any space.

Activity

Talk to your partner to find out something about him/her, so you can introduce your partner to a group. If everyone already knows everyone else, make up answers, as if you were another person. Find out a prearranged number of things about your partner without asking any questions. Each person in turn introduces the partner.

Suggestions

Introduce topics that can be commented on, rather than making statements that are complete in themselves.

Introduce objects which evoke responses. Try to establish age without asking "how old." Find out likes and dislikes without asking direct questions.

Questions

What is the difference between finding out information through questioning and not questioning?

How do you feel responding to direct questions?

Do you prefer asking or not asking questions?

How do you feel when you have to introduce someone to a group?

How do environmental changes affect ease or rapport?

RELAXATION (I)

Purpose

To relax

To evoke images

To provide respite from tension and fatigue

Participants and Space

Any number, space to sit without touching.

Activity

Sit in a comfortable position on the floor or in a chair, with your eyes closed, and arms resting on thighs. Think of air being let out of a balloon slowly and evenly. Let the body sink, getting heavier and heavier. Let the mind wander, and explore the images that arise (clouds, flowers floating on water, puff-balls in the air, bubbles have been suggested). Breathing may begin to change, so the inhalation is longer and more active than the exhalation, which is passive. A pause may develop between exhalation and the next inhalation. This means the pattern of breathing while sleeping is effected, and is a sign of deepening relaxation.

When it is time to resume activity, open your eyes slowly. Stretch the whole body gently, from head to toe; yawn. Rise to standing.

Suggestions

This relaxation activity is the easiest to introduce. Young children often get silly when asked to lie down; older people feel self-conscious. Space may be a problem, too. At the end of the relaxation period, have everyone resume a sitting position, keeping their eyes closed, and share images that may have come to mind. There should be no attempt to make everyone feel they *had* to have an image, or that they have to share it.

Questions

Can you watch your breathing without changing its pattern?

What effect does relaxation work have on what you do afterward?

Does your body weight feel different during this activity?

How do you feel doing this kind of exercise?

RELAXATION (II)

Purpose

To relax

To provide respite from tension and fatigue

To explore the effect of breathing on muscular tension

Participants and Space

Any number, with space for everyone to lie down without touching each other.

Activity

This activity can be done individually, but it is more effective, especially in the beginning, to work with a leader.

Lie on your back, arms out slightly to the side, palms up, head to one side or on a pillow. Work on a rug or mat, if available.

These are the directions for the leader to give the group:

"Feel your body becoming very heavy; let it sink into the floor. Begin to check each part of the body: feet, calves, thighs, stomach, chest, shoulders, head, mouth, eyes, arms, fingers; feel the tension and weight begin to ebb out. Let go of everything. Now, without changing it, monitor your breathing. Begin to lengthen your inhalation. Let the exhalation happen automatically. Pause before the next inhalation. Work easily, without forcing."

The exercise can stop here, and people can stretch to get out of it, or they can go on to the next part: "Working one side of the body at a time, flex and tense the left foot, keeping the right foot relaxed. Then tense the right foot, and relax the left. Repeat until all parts of the body have been worked, including eyes, mouth, cheeks and forehead. (Eyes are usually very tense and should be checked often.) When the whole body has been tensed and relaxed, check the breathing again. Hold this position (beginners, 30 seconds; more advanced, up to ten minutes); then slowly begin to stretch. Stand up slowly."

Suggestions

Very tense people should put a pillow under their knees. Slow, soothing music may help, at a low volume. The leader should speak in a calm, unemotional voice, low in pitch. Try *not* to let people go to sleep.

Questions

After practicing this for a while, your body may develop a mind set. As you assume the relaxed position, do your muscles begin to let go without conscious direction?

Have you tried this activity when you have difficulty going to sleep at night?

What do you feel like if you forget to stretch afterward?

RELAXATION (III) *[from a workshop by Robert Nadeau]*
Purpose

To relax

To work cooperatively

To explore the effect of images as an aid to relaxation

Participants and Space

Partners; space to lie down without touching each other.

Activity

Lie down on your back, arms slightly out, eyes closed, head to one side. Your partner should sit with legs apart, at your head, so the partner can gently place both hands on your shoulders. Fingers should be spread around the collarbone rather than on it. The partner should assume a comfortable sitting position, so shifting is not necessary, since this would ruin the effect. The leader should use a watch with a second hand, to know how long people work. The leader should give the following directions in a calm, unemotional voice when everyone is settled. (Each direction should take one-half a minute, and be repeated twice for a total of two minutes.) Tell the person lying down to think about a cool, clear, calm, deep pool of water. Tell the person sitting to think about the sun; warm, soothing, radiating energy. The intervals between the directions can be extended gradually to 5 or 10 minutes as the group becomes more experienced. When the first two-minute period is over, tell the sitting person to remove his/her hands. This should take at least 30 seconds. When removed, the sitting person should slide away from the partner. Both should stretch very thoroughly and very, very slowly, stand up. Reverse positions.

Suggestions

Keep the spoken directions easy and smooth. Quiet music may help. With practice, this becomes easier, and initial silliness disappears, especially if the leader works as a member of the group. After both partners have tried both positions, there is a tendency to talk about the experience. Encourage this; if desired, share with the group.

Questions

Which position do you prefer?

How do you feel when the hands are removed from your body?

What are some other images that might work?

SECTION II

After doing some of the activities in the first section, the group will be able to work more openly. Although the activities in this section are more complicated and challenging, they function on individual levels. Their complexity can be broken down, and phases of an activity can be worked on separately.

The activities in this section explore emotional response more directly than before. It helps to state problems very clearly; this will reduce self-consciousness and provide a supportive environment. The ability to work openly does not happen all at once; this is a gradual process, and different people move at different rates.

It is easy to lose patience at this stage, because the teacher can feel a person's readiness and not know how to help. Often it is best to let the student decide for him/herself. It is analogous to teaching a child how to walk: for a long time the child holds on to the adult with one finger, receiving little support, yet unable to let go. Only when the child is secure is it possible to stand and walk alone.

These exercises encourage the student's independence, and help give the group a good basis for evaluations.

Continue to explore the activities in the first section, so you can see how much you have learned by your ability to solve familiar problems. Often simpler activities offer great challenges for creative development because you are forced to draw upon resources deep within yourself.

It is important to continually point out progress in order to avoid discouragement. After initial break-throughs, progress is less dramatic and therefore less noticeable.

WORKING WITH NON-VERBAL CUES

Purpose
To work from non-verbal cues

To work cooperatively

To make the imagined "real"

Participants and Space
Partners or small groups; space in which to move.

Activity
Working in partners, one person should start to lift an imaginary object. The partner helps lift and put it down, following cues received from the person who started the activity.

Suggestions
The object can be light, heavy, small, large, gooey, smelly, expensive, fragile, dangerous, and so on.

Questions
What if your partner were incapacitated (broken leg, arm)?

Without words, how do you communicate: dangerous, fragile, or other qualifications?

How do you respond if your partner begins to get the wrong idea?

What situations can you think of which go beyond putting the object down and lifting it up?

What happens if you cannot put the object down, if it flies away or rolls out of reach?

FOLLOW THE LEADER (II)

Purpose

To work cooperatively

To develop sensitivity to nuances of sound and movement

To improve peripheral vision

Participants and Space

Small groups of 4 or 5, with space for each group to work in without disturbing others.

Activity

Non-verbally, one person in each group establishes a direction. The rest of the group follows the direction, but not necessarily the same movement. The direction can be: up, down, in, out, moving to a particular place, or a combination. When everyone is doing the same thing, a new person should establish a different direction. Use sounds to make the movement more interesting. Try complementary sounds and rhythms.

Suggestions

The same activity can be used to explore levels of tension, sounds (eyes closed and open), focus (with eyes and other parts of the body), or any combination. Work with and without physical contact. If used, try making contact with parts of the body other than the hands.

Questions

Does working in a particular way give you ideas for stories?

Do you find it easier to work without verbal directions?

Do some people tend to dominate the group?

Does everyone make sure each person gets a chance to lead?

Which is most difficult for you to follow: sounds, tension levels, direction or focus?

Can you work without paying attention to other groups?

Does working this way affect the group's feelings about each other?

FINISHING WHAT SOMEONE STARTS

Purpose

To work from non-verbal cues

To work cooperatively

To work imaginatively and spontaneously

Participants and Space

Partners or any number (the higher the number, the more difficult); space in which to move.

Activity

One person (or more if desired) starts an activity, real or imagined, which cannot be finished without help from another person or people. A partner is non-verbally invited to help, and they finish the task together. Do not discuss beforehand what activity will be undertaken. The initiator could start to lift a heavy box, dig a hole, fly a kite in an increasingly strong wind, try to get something which is out of reach, or any other appropriate activity. When the first activity is completed, partners should reverse roles.

Suggestions

The invitation can be proffered with eyes, gibberish, by hand, leg; or the partner can invite him/herself. Experiment with different qualifications: needing but not wanting to ask for help; wanting help in a hurry, and so on. Continue the activity after the initial task is accomplished. Let each member of the group take the initiative. Have two people work and a third interrupt.

Questions

What kind of activities are difficult to join?

How do you ask for help non-verbally so your partner knows what to do and how to do it?

If your partner does not understand what you are doing, how does it make you feel? Does it effect your work the next time?

Are there times in real life when this type of situation might arise?

How would you work if you did not want to show your feelings?

FREE FALLS (I)

Purpose

To develop physical courage, acknowledging fear

To develop physical trust in the group

To learn how to catch people safely

To work cooperatively and supportively

Participants and Space

Groups of at least seven; space in which to fall. If possible, work on mats or rugs, especially in the beginning. (A 100-lb. person should be caught by six people of at least the same weight.)

This activity is not recommended for children under 12, unless there are adults to supervise closely.

Activity

Standing on a desk, platform, or level at least 4 to 5 feet high, fall (do not dive) into the arms of people who have formed two lines and are holding each other's wrists. As you are caught, the group should give with the impact, bending knees slightly. Remaining rigid is less comfortable and less safe for the faller and the catchers. The fall should be executed with face front, arms overhead by ears, and the body extended as much as possible. Each person should have a turn. An extra person should stand at the head of the two lines just in case the person falls too far forward.

Suggestions

With experience, people can vary the falls, falling backward (hands by the sides) and sideward (arms up to protect the ears). Slowly increase the height of the faller and of the level from which he/she falls; the higher, the heavier. If people are afraid, they should be encouraged to express their fears and start from low levels. People with back or other injuries should check with their doctor before doing this.

Encourage people to share their feelings about this experience. Some fine paintings and drawings have resulted from people expressing how they felt about this activity.

Questions

How did you feel the first time you fell forward? Was it different when you fell backward or sideward?

Did being caught by the group affect your feelings about them?

How did you feel when a very fearful person was finally able to fall?

If you are afraid, can you express this fear? How?

FREE FALLS (II)

Purpose

To develop physical courage, acknowledging fear

To develop physical trust in the group

To learn how to catch people safely

To work cooperatively and supportively

Participants and Space

Groups of at least 9, with 8 people to catch one person; space in which to fall. Ceilings should be at least 12 feet. If possible, work on mats or rugs. This is not recommended for young or small people.

Activity

Four people should stand next to each other, shoulder to shoulder. Four more people should stand behind them in the same position. Start by having a small person (the ninth) lie across the arms of the front four people. On count three, the front four should toss the person over their heads, into the arms of the four standing behind them. With experience, have the front four re-group behind the back four, and the back four can continue to toss the person behind them. Repeat the procedure as long as there is space, achieving a wave effect. Each person in the group should have a chance to be thrown and to catch.

Suggestions

As the group becomes more confident, there is a tendency for wildness to develop. Take a breathing break if this occurs, to avoid possibility of injury. If the person being thrown wishes to stop, respect his/her feelings. Work with eyes open and closed. Try using this as part of a dramatic situation. Encourage the group to share feelings about throwing and being thrown.

Questions

How does the experience of throwing compare with being thrown?

How do you feel working with someone bigger or smaller than you?

If you are big or heavy, how did you feel being caught?

How does it feel to be thrown repeatedly?

Were you more comfortable with your eyes open or closed?

Do you like this experience? After doing it several times, do your feelings change?

MAKE A SHAPE, USE IT
Purpose

To work imaginatively

To work spontaneously

To make something new from something familiar

To develop spatial and kinesthetic awareness

Participants and Space

Any number, any space.

This activity is difficult for young children; they need to see examples worked out by the group.

Older people get too involved in reality and are easily stymied; it may help them to work as a group also.

Activity

One person makes a shape and freezes. (Choose positions that can be maintained without discomfort.) A second person finds a way, with movement and sound, to use the first person's shape; then the two people freeze in the resulting position. A third person uses their shape, and all three freeze when finished. Repeat the process until everybody has worked, or no-one can think of anything new to add.

Suggestions

This activity may be repeated many times. Most people find it funny and relaxing. If the group is shy, start with volunteers. With experience, people should be able to respond to any shape or size. Try to work spontaneously. Too much thinking can be counter-productive; do not look for inner logic. Self-censorship is destructive because it denies the individual a chance to explore new ideas.

Questions

What gives you ideas on how to transform the shape?

How do you connect images to ideas?

How do you feel when it is your turn to alter the shape?

After doing this activity a few times, do you feel differently about it, and does it become easier to find ideas?

Can you try this activity looking at cloud formations or patterns in the water when the wind blows? Where else?

WORKING WITH A PARACHUTE

Parachutes are available in most playground equipment catalogues. They come in different sizes, colors and weights, and offer a wonderful variety of experiences for all ages.

Young children, needing each other to make the parachute soar, learn how to work cooperatively. They can also experience concepts such as: over, on top of, under, round, and flat.

Older people can also benefit from working with a parachute, because it stimulates fantasy and sensual response.

Purpose
To explore working with an unusual prop

To work cooperatively

To use a prop to stimulate fantasy

To use a prop to explore responses with various media

Participants and Space
Any number, large open space (very high ceiling, or out of doors).

Before working with a parachute, young children should practice activities such as *moving on and off center*, and *fast starts* and *sudden stops*.

Activity
There are an infinite number of ways to use the parachute, depending on the age and size of the group. Usually people will suggest ideas as they go along. Some ways to start: On a count of three, holding the parachute, throw it up in the air. Then, on a count of three, let go. When the parachute is coming down, get under it and feel how it falls on you. Wave the parachute about three feet off the floor while some people run in it. Get under the parachute and move around in it; those watching make sounds.

Paint the way you felt working with a parachute. Make up a story based on these feelings, or create an improvisation.

Questions

How do you feel when, holding on to the parachute, it soars?

How do you feel when it falls on top of you?

What do you not like about working with a parachute?

Have you ever talked to someone who jumped out of a plane with one?

What might you do with a parachute that no-one has thought of?

WORKING WITH OBSTACLES (II)

Purpose

To develop kinesthetic awareness

To sharpen response to auditory stimuli

To work cooperatively

To experience working without vision

To trust perception of self and group

Participants and Space

Any number, any size space.

Young children will feel more comfortable in smaller spaces.

Activity

Divide the group into small groups of three or four. Have one small group either leave the room, close eyes, or put on blindfolds. The remaining people should create group obstacles, each with its own sound and shape. Give each small group-obstacle a number, but do not arrange the groups in numerical sequence. The more jumbled the numbers (for example: 6, 3, 2,

5, 1, 4), the more difficult the experience. Have each person in the blindfolded group go through all the obstacles. Everyone should know beforehand the total number of obstacles. When they have heard all the numbers, have them remove their blindfolds and look at what they moved through. Each blindfolded group should have different obstacles to maneuver.

Suggestions

If the noise level gets too loud, suggest the sounds be body sounds rather than vocal sounds. A sighted person should always be watching, to prevent anyone from straying. Make sure that people treat each other carefully, since excitement in this exercise can lead to rough-housing.

Questions

When you looked at the obstacles, how did they compare to what they felt like while you were going through them?

Did you feel the obstacles were helping, making your life difficult, or neither?

Do you like working without being able to see where you are going? Why?

DIARIES

Purpose

To record feelings and changes in feelings

To gain perspective of one's feelings

To explore how working with feelings affects feelings

Participants

Any number.

Activity

Make a large cardboard book, at least 8½"x11," preferably larger. When you feel strongly about something, record it in the diary using paints, crayons, charcoal, words or photographs. Stories, poems, plays, word pictures and cartoons are all possibilities. After you have kept the diary for a set period of time, review what has been recorded, the media used, and your responses to it. Have the group share responses, discuss changes that have occurred. When common themes appear, suggest ways that stories, poems, pictures and other entries might be explored further.

Suggestions

It is difficult to have perspective about yourself and your feelings in the middle of an emotional experience. Keeping a diary helps you do this. Often patterns begin to emerge, offering valuable insights. At the very least, a diary will help people who feel they have nothing to say, or do not know what to do. Perhaps keep a school diary and a home diary, to you can see how environment affects feelings.

Questions

What effect could keeping a diary have on your feelings?

What can you record in one medium that would not work as well in another?

If you have kept a diary for some time, what do you think about it?

If you have shared part of your diary with others, what effect does their response have on you?

Do you want to share all or part of your diary with someone?
Are you able to record all of your feelings: those you might be
    ashamed of, as well as those that are "perfectly natural"?
Do you see a pattern in your emotional responses?
Are you aware of most feelings most of the time?

USING FRUSTRATION TO STIMULATE INVENTION

There are always frustrations which arise while working: not
enough time, too little space, not enough money. Encourage the
group to use frustration as stimulation for creative response; the
total experience will be far more productive. The following example illustrates this.

A woman donated some lovely colored felt to a group of
fourth-grade students who were putting together a play. The
material was going to be used again, so the woman stipulated that
it not be sewed or cut. What first seemed impossible became a
source of hilarity as the group stapled, folded and shaped the felt
into costumes. The costumes were imaginative, easy to make, and
unique.

Purpose
    To encourage inventiveness
    To overcome and transform frustration
    To be open to, and explore, different possibilities

Participants and Space
    Any number; space with levels, boxes and mats if possible.

Activity
    Divide into small groups, with each developing a short im-
provisation. Share these with the total group. Have the people

watching suggest new extenuating circumstances, such as: your working time is cut in half; one person has hurt a leg; everyone has developed laryngitis; the space is filled with obstacles. Have each group work with the new qualification. Discuss as a group the effect of the qualification on the improvisation.

Suggestions

As frustrations arise in the work, try using them. Have each student try to work this way in daily living, and share results with the group. Explore sources of frustrations and ways they can be altered.

Questions

What happens to your frustration if you confront and work with it?

How can you use this in daily living?

What happens to group relations when you use frustration creatively?

Do you have a notion of perfection in regard to living and where you live? How would it be if this were realized?

What part does frustration play in shaping you as a person?

Explain how you consider frustration to be bad, good, or what?

Think of the most frustrating thing that could happen to you. How could you transform it into a force for growth?

Does working this way affect your ideas? How?

USING EXPERIENCE TO ALTER EXPERIENCE

This exercise was suggested by a third-grade teacher. As she and her students were visiting an indoor garden with a tin roof, a sudden thunder and lightning storm broke out, causing a terrifying din on the roof. The children were frightened, and the teacher began to lose control of the group. Trying to calm them, she got them into a circle and asked a few to volunteer to show her and the rest of the class how they would move if they were frightened. Some children got up immediately, and began to move and make sounds. Soon the whole group was moving "as if" they were very frightened.

To give them a rest, the teacher asked them to sit down, and tell what kinds of situations frightened them. After everyone had been given a chance to speak, she asked them to work alone or in small groups, and act out a frightening situation, using movement and sound.

Later, when the children were sharing their work, one child said, "It's hard to be frightened and act frightened at the same time." By confronting and working through their fear, the children were able to share some strong emotions and control them. After this work, though the storm continued, the children were no longer upset by it.

Specific situations, such as the one above, cannot be predicted, but general ways of working can be suggested. It helps to have good rapport between the group and its leader; it also helps to do some of this work together before using a spontaneous set of circumstances. Even a novice leader and an inexperienced group can use the moment if people are sensitive to each other's feelings and emotional states.

Purpose

To use an emotional moment to explore feelings

To become sensitive to the variety of feelings from an experience

To work imaginatively

To work cooperatively and compassionately

Participants and Space

Any number, any space.

Activity

Suppose someone tells the group that, because of noise, work must stop and everybody leave. Most people are angry, some are frightened, a few are relieved because the atmosphere was chaotic, and a few are glad because they had not been enjoying the work. Ways of handling the situation depend on specific circumstances. One would be to present an appeal to whoever bid them stop. People could draw up a petition and sign it. Another way would be to create a drama showing what they had been learning, and how they were enjoying themselves. They could sing their dissatisfaction (presenting a miniature opera); they could use paint, clay, sound, movement and present this to the authority.

Suggestions

The process of looking at an experience objectively, while you are in the middle of it, helps you and the group respond with better control. Being able to look at alternatives when you are already involved helps you make a more intelligent or desirable response. It is a valuable experience to make yourself see more than one choice at a time when you ordinarily would not think of choices.

Questions

How does working with an experience while you are being affected by it alter your feelings?

How does this type of experience affect you later, in similar situations?

How do you feel about considering alternatives in the middle of a charged experience?

What kind of changes occur between members of the group and between the leader and the group?

How do you feel about watching yourself respond to a situation?

Does the watching itself alter the response?

How do you feel about yourself after working this way? Are there changes?

If you are afraid of something, and purposely make yourself move the way the fear dictates, how does this affect the original feeling of fear?

POSING PROBLEMS

Purpose

To learn to ask questions that stimulate activity

To decentralize the source of stimulation

To share the responsibility of providing stimulation

Participants and Space

Any number, large open space if possible.

Activity

Have each person pose a problem that can be answered only by action. Begin questions with the following: "How many different ways can you . . ." and end them with types of movement, such as:

1 move across the floor using two hands and one foot?
2 leap, flinging your arms in the air, your face toward the ceiling?
3 leap, with your focus on the ground?
4 swirl so that your arms seem to lift of their own accord?
5 move slowly across the floor so others can hardly tell whether your body is moving at all?
6 roll and come to a sudden stop?
7 leap holding a partner's hand?
8 move to words such as *mashed potatoes* or *pusillanimous*?
9 move very close to, but without letting your body touch, the floor?
10 swirl backward and come to a sudden stop?

Suggestions

The whole group should work out individual solutions, avoiding comparison. There should be a premium placed on solving the same problem differently. Ask questions which explore sound, rhythm, line, poetry and shape.

Questions

Which questions make you feel challenged? Bored?

What questions arise from the questioner's lack of knowledge?

How do these differ from those designed to see what you know?

How do open-ended questions make you feel?

Do you think the quality of a question is related to knowledge?

Can you learn to ask good questions? If so, how?

What kind of environment supports the asking of challenging and meaningful questions?

ASKING "WHAT WOULD HAPPEN IF?" (I)

Purpose

To explore possiblity

To learn to ask stimulating questions

To encourage incongruity and absurdity

To use existing material to create new material

Participants and Space

Any number, any space.

Activity

Have each person choose an interesting photograph, painting, story or play. (These can be brought in ahead of time by members of the group, but you do not have to use what you brought in if something appeals to you more.) It is fine if several people want to work with the same thing. After you have chosen your piece, write down five questions starting with "What would happen if . . ." Each question should open a realm of possiblity: a new ending, a character with a different action, a different set of circumstances. If several people are working on the same piece, have them arrive at their questions independently. When finished, have some volunteers share their questions, while the group looks at the original source. If you use a story, give the group a brief outline. After you present your questions, have the group suggest others.

Suggestions

Learning to ask stimulating questions is an important part of the creative process. Once you learn to do this, anything is possible. Discuss which questions help and which do not. Questions starting with "Why did you do . . . " or "What did you mean by . . . " usually put the person on the defensive. A better approach is to ask those watching: "Were all your questions answered? Were there some things you would like to know more about? What other possibilities might be explored?" Try *not* to ask judgemental questions. Critical analysis comes much later, after people have learned to respond and experiment openly.

Questions

What kinds of questions encourage you? Which discourage you?

What questions make the person asking seem so knowledgeable that you would like to scream?

What is the purpose of asking questions?

Could you ask a question in a large hall before a big audience?

What atmosphere encourages the asking of questions?

ASKING "WHAT WOULD HAPPEN IF?" (II)

Purpose

To experience possibility

To be open to exploration, incongruity and absurdity

To be spontaneous and flexible

Participants and Space

Any number, any space.

Activity

Divide into small groups. Each group should choose one of the paintings, photos, stories or plays used to stimulate the asking of questions. Working with old or new questions, explore the possiblities they suggest. It is not necessary to choose only one possibility; work with several. Focus on an open point of view. Encourage absurdity and incongruity. When the groups are ready, share the questions and explorations.

Suggestions

Ask the group to discuss how this type of questioning could be used in daily living. Share feelings about working this way. Find out how important discoveries in science, medicine and other disciplines came about. If you only deal with the known, how will new discoveries be made? Discuss how you feel about trying unknown things.

Questions

How do you prepare to work with something that is unknown?
Do you feel comfortable and satisfied with what you know?
Is there any impetus to go beyond this?
How much can you predict about your life in the next 10 years?
What would you like to see happen? Can you make it happen?
How can you use open-ended questions in your own life?
How do open-ended questions affect the person in the leadership role (teacher, principal, counselor)?

What is the difference between open and closed questions?

How can closed questions be used to make people feel ignorant?

What is the difference in the role played by the person who asks an open, and the person who asks a closed, question?

WHAT CAN (CAN NOT) IT BE?

Purpose

To develop critical thinking

To look for common elements

To develop imagination

Participants and Space

Any number, any space.

Activity

Start with a piece of crumpled net or newspaper and ask the group, "What could this shape be? What could it not be?" Have part of the group make a machine and ask the same questions. Play some sounds on a tape recorder, or have the group identify something with their eyes closed, again asking the two questions. The point is to discover what knowledge is necessary to identify something. By asking, "What could it not be," the group learns a great deal about how narrow most people's range of thinking is, how limited their imagination. More importantly, the group will learn to improve their own critical thinking.

Suggestions

When answers are offered to what something could or could not be, ask *why*, or how the person arrived at the conclusion.

Often things which seem illogical at first hearing are not only logical but imaginative. A teacher asked her class to describe infinity. A child volunteered the answer that infinity was like the label on a peanut-butter jar, and was sent to the principal for being rude. The principal questioned the child about his response and was told: "On the label is a picture of a jar of peanut butter, and there must be a label on that jar, and one on the jar in the picture of the picture. Isn't that infinity?"

Questions

What makes you decide what something could or could not be?

How imaginative are your responses?

How do you decide the crucial factor determining what something could not be?

Do you prefer figuring out what something could be or what something could not be?

SOUND AND MOVEMENT CONVERSATIONS

Purpose

To explore the effect of sound on feeling

To explore nonverbal communication

To feel comfortable with absurdity

Participants and Space

Pairs working in a good sized space.

Activity

One person initiates the activity by making some sounds. The partner responds to these sounds by moving the way the sounds make him/her feel. The initiator then executes a movement to which the partner responds in sounds. When ready, switch roles. Words can be used, but not to make sense. Work with a few partners. Try a 3- or 4-way conversation. Share work and responses with the total group.

Suggestions

If the group finds it difficult to get started, play a taped conversation (that is very animated) at the wrong speeds, too slow and too fast. See how different levels and distance affect the response. Try working in a darkened room or in a room with an echo to see how it alters the experience. Do people seem to be having real conversations? Try combining sound and movement. Work with varying levels of intensity.

Questions

How do you feel doing this activity? Why?

Do you find yourself and your partner trying to "make sense" in your conversation?

How wide a range of response are you free to explore?

Does this activity seem silly to you?

What does it take for a silly activity not to seem so silly?

What does "silly" mean to you?

How does age affect the notion of silliness?

How do you feel if someone says you are acting silly? Do you care?

Does your response to the person calling you silly depend on who that person is? Why or why not?

SHARPENING LISTENING SKILLS

Purpose

To give clear directions

To respond to directions without using vision

To improve ability to listen

To use touch to determine spatial orientation

Participants and Space

Any number sitting on the floor with space in which to work.

Activity

Have people cut colored paper into predetermined shapes and sizes. If desired, apply textures to shapes to add complexity. Each person should also have a large sheet of paper and glue or paste. When all the shapes are ready, everybody should be blindfolded (including the leader).* If desired, half the group can work while the other half quietly watches, then reverse. The leader gives directions to those blindfolded, telling them where to place each shape on their individual sheet of paper. Shapes may be superimposed or slightly off the edge of the paper. When all the shapes have been used, take off blindfolds and have the people look at their work.

Suggestions

When the group looks at the finished paper, avoid making people feel badly whose shapes are incorrectly placed. Instead, discuss the problem of listening.

This activity can also be done with line drawing. Draw a small circle (size of a quarter) in the upper left hand corner of a piece of paper. If you use cardboard and a ballpoint pen, you

*People with learning disabilities may find this activity too difficult to do blindfolded; let them work without blindfolds, by themselves.

will be able to feel the imprint of the pen, and it will help orient you in relation to the rest of the space.

This activity can be made even more difficult by using three dimensional space. Give people who have been blindfolded directions, telling them to put specific objects in specific places.

Questions

How much do you depend on eyesight to follow directions?

Is this activity difficult for you, or is it easy?

In general, do you depend more upon what you hear than on what you see?

How accurate is your spatial perception when you cannot rely on vision?

Is it harder to place an object somewhere in a room than to put a shape somewhere on a sheet of paper? Why?

How do you feel having to rely on hearing and touch rather than on vision?

How acute is your ability to distinguish upper, lower, square, rectangle, circle, when you can not depend on vision?

USING SPACE IMAGINATIVELY

Purpose

To explore how space can serve as stimulus

To experience the effect of different spaces on individuals

To use difficult spaces imaginatively

Participants and Space

Any number, depending on the size and availability of different spaces. Young children should work only in those spaces that have been checked beforehand, and do not have self-locking doors, poisonous cleaning supplies, unsafe tree limbs, and so on. This is a good activity for people of all ages.

Activity

Find spaces* that you would not ordinarily work in, such as custodian's closets, basements, trees, fences, offices, swings, caves, and so on. When many spaces have been found, share them with the total group, and list those that are usable and safe. Depending on space, work individually, in pairs or in small groups, and create an improvisation using the space and the feelings it evokes as stimuli. Try to absorb and communicate the quality of the space, so when the work is shared, those watching will understand the effect the space had on you. Have each person try several different spaces. Share work.

Suggestions

It will affect the work if the space is filled with obstacles, very small, dark, bad-smelling, high off the ground. Try to share the sensation that affected you most deeply, relying less on verbal description than on physicalization. If several people have used the same space, share the work before comments or questions begin. Focus on how differently the same space can affect different people, rather than trying to standardize a response. Put together several experiences.

Questions

How does being in a small space affect you?
Does it matter if the small space is inside or outside?
What spaces intrigue you? What spaces comfort you?
What spaces frighten, frustrate or repel you?

* Use pictures of spaces as well as actual spaces.

Does this activity affect the way you look at space in daily living? If so, how?

Does this activity stimulate the creation of stories, poems or paintings? If it does not, why not?

WORKING IN ALTERED SPACES (I)

Purpose

To explore the effect of space on feelings

To be sensitive to the effects of changing space

To work imaginatively

To become aware of the differences of response

Participants and Space

Small groups working in various kinds of spaces

Activity

Start with a space in which everyone feels comfortable, and alter it in some way: turn out the lights, fill the room with objects, or play strange sounds. Have each group physicalize how the altered space makes them feel. Stress that each person in the group work from his/her own feelings, rather than merging all feelings into one common response. If the group is responsible, send small groups into some small spaces, such as the custodian's closet; also send them into the biggest room, to a tree, or into the basement.

Suggestions

Have the group suggest ways of making familiar space unfamiliar. Share work with the larger group, expaining what it was like to be in the dark, in a small place, and so on.

Questions

What do you take for granted in the spaces you work, play, live in?

What changes would be necessary to alter your feelings about these spaces?

Are there some spaces that make you fearful, joyful, or powerful? What is the spatial element involved in each case?

How did your feelings differ when people worked close to you or far away? Did you prefer one? If so, why?

GROUP STATUES

Purpose

To work imaginatively

To work cooperatively

To explore the effect of position and contiguity on imagination

To work with multiple possiblities

Participants and Space

Any number, large open space.

Young children may have trouble with this activity.

Activity

Have one or two people work with a group of six or seven, forming them into a group statue. When formed, those watching should suggest, if the statue were alive, what, who and where it might be, and what might happen next. The group statue should explore all or several of the suggested possibilities. If the group runs out of ideas, those watching could offer qualifications such as: a giant is roaming the land; it is getting very cold, people are hungry. When one group has finished, another group should work. Groups can work simultaneously, but a great deal can be learned by watching others. The emphasis should be on the process of exploration, not the finished product. The statue can represent an event (planting a flag), a place (classroom), or an emotion (people being shoved into line at gun-point). The statue could be suggested by previous work or experience.

Suggestions

If someone has been in a difficult situation, let the person mold a statue re-creating part of this situation, and see how alternatives could be developed. If desired, equal numbers of people can form and be formed, so the groups can reverse roles. Words should not be used if possible. Try having the statue group keep their eyes closed. Sounds can be made by the statue, or given by the sculptors. Use this exercise to stimulate writing, poetry, or plays by having the statue be the beginning or end.

Questions

What ways can you form statues which involve giving a direction and having the statue come out of a direction (swirl in a small space and stop when I clap)?

How do you discover what the total statue is if you are a part of it, and cannot see the whole?

What effect does a change in dynamics, level, or focus have?

How do you feel trying to create when people are watching?

WORKING OBJECTIVELY TO EXPLORE EMOTION

Purpose

To physicalize feelings comfortably

To work sensitively

To explore non-verbal communication

Participants and Space

Any number, any space.

Activity

Think up a mechanical problem, such as: go toward your partner; go away from your partner; pass your partner with one of you not noticing the other; pass your partner with neither of you noticing. Qualify the experience by working slowly, quickly, one slow one fast, one with tension, one with irregular rhythms, and so on. Let the emotional response come out of the work. If none is evoked, just keep on working with a variety of problems, focus, levels, dynamics, pace and tension.

Suggestions

Have the group make up a list of 20 usable problems. Write them on separate pieces of paper and put them in a box. People should draw from the box if they run out of ideas. Take one problem and explore multiple solutions. Have everyone work on the same problem, to explore variety. After working non-verbally, see how words affect the work. Share work with the group. Try not to make prior decisions about how to solve a problem; work spontaneously.

Questions

How do you focus on yourself and a partner at the same time?

How do you "listen" to your feelings in order to know how
you feel?

How do you let the emotional response out rather than forcing
a response you do not feel?

How do you work "genuinely" rather than "play-acting"
when dealing with imagined feeling?

What are some mechanical problems that are simple enough to
allow a great variety of exploration?

What is the difference between a mechanical problem and an
emotional problem (the latter: you are crying because your
dog died)?

Which is more difficult to solve, a mechanical or an emotional
problem?

EXPANDING SENSORY AWARENESS
Purpose
To sharpen the senses of touch, hearing, smell, taste

To experience dependency and interdependency

To experience trust or distrust

Participants and Space
Any number, any space.

If the group is very young or hard to handle, work in small
groups with good supervision.

Activity
Before meeting, prepare an environment that includes smells
(isolated in paper bags), textures, levels, sounds (on tape or
live), things to eat and to drink. Blindfold half the group. In

pairs, one leading the blindfolded other one, go through the room giving the partner as rich and safe an experience as possible. When the blindfolded person has been led through, reverse roles until everyone has experienced leading and being led. Share work.

Suggestions

One person should stand apart and act as supervisor. If people work too quickly, play slow, soft music. Each person should be blindfolded anywhere from 1 to 30 minutes, depending on age and ability to concentrate. After some experience, lead people out of the room, into other parts of the indoor or outdoor environment. Explore what things *seem like* or *could be*, rather than just what things *are*.

Questions

Do you prefer leading or being led? Why?

How do you feel when you can see after being blindfolded?

How long do you think you could function without vision?

How accurate are your senses of touch, taste and smell?

How well can you remember location of objects when you can not see?

Do you feel more imaginative using or not using vision? Why?

How do you feel depending on someone else?

When leading someone else, are you tempted to put the person into a dangerous situation?

Do you trust everyone to lead you? Why or why not?

How does the group feel about each other after this activity?

Could you function in your own house blindfolded?

MOVING IN TRANSFORMED SPACE

Purpose

To explore the effect of imagery on movement

To work imaginatively

To use imagery to stimulate the imagination

Participants and Space

Any number, large open space.

Activity

Have the group move, individually. Qualify movements with suggestions such as: "Now you are moving on ice," or, "Pretend you are swimming in molasses." These qualifications can be suggested by the people watching or the people moving. Divide the group into smaller groups of 3 or 4. Have each smaller group choose one thing to work with (more than one can choose the same thing), and develop an improvisation based on how moving this way makes them feel. In addition to, or instead of the improvisation, each group could make a group painting of how this makes them feel. When finished, share work.

Suggestions

Try working with and without physical contact. When using physical contact, work with parts of the body other than arms and hands. What would happen if people were walking on ice, touching feet, heads, or eyelashes? Try finger-painting to express feelings, using other parts of the body than the fingers.

Questions

What makes you look and feel different, moving on ice or in molasses? Would it help if you tried moving in molasses?

How do you feel finger-painting with elbows, toes, or some other part of your body?

How do you feel when asked to do or react to something bizarre? Are you easily embarrassed? Why?

What is the difference between doing something strange and having people think you silly, and doing the same thing and having people envy your daring, freedom, or inventiveness?

ESTABLISHING ENVIRONMENT (I)

Purpose

To become more conscious of one's environment

To physicalize one's feelings about an environment

To work cooperatively

To respond imaginatively to non-verbal cues

Participants and Space

Small groups in a space large enough to move in and around.

Activity

Have groups of four to six physicalize the kind of imaginary environment they are in. Without words, spectators should be able to tell whether it is hot or cold; if the terrain is hilly or flat; if there are trees, rocks, streams, or other creatures. It should be clear if the group is comfortable or not.

Suggestions

In the beginning, it is best to work physically, with the group responding as a whole. Those watching should ask questions

leading to a more complex physical description. The more details supplied by the group, the richer the experience.

Questions

What kinds of things are easily physicalized? Which are more difficult? Why?

What things in an environment make you feel comfortable, strange, anxious, afraid or relaxed?

Are you aware of the extent to which you are influenced by your physical environment? Does working on this activity change your awareness? If so, how?

What are the differences between the way you respond to an environment, and the way a friend, a person with whom you are not friendly, or a person in authority responds to it?

Why do you think these differences occur?

USING EYE CONTACT

Purpose

To focus on the role eyes play in non-verbal communication

To explore ideas and feelings conveyed by the eyes

To use the eyes to establish emotional contact

Participants and Space

Any even number, any space.

Activity

Have everybody move in space until a signal to freeze is given. Using only your eyes, make contact with another person. Remain in contact until everyone has a partner. On a pre-arranged signal, go toward your partner in a manner suggested by the position in which you looked at each other. Greet each other non-verbally in a consistent manner. The whole group should then repeat the activity, each person working with a new partner. After trying it several times, come together as a group and share experiences. Some may volunteer immediately, others may prefer not to talk. Discuss how effective the eyes are, and the ideas and feelings that were and could be communicated.

Suggestions

Try making contact with 2 or 3 others, instead of one. Start from strange positions, partially hidden by objects or other people, and work to different kinds of music, including environmental music. Make some tapes to provide stimulation. If some people cannot find a partner, have the group make suggestions. Teen-agers may be very self-conscious at first, but become interested after a few tries, and get past their self-consciousness. Sometimes this activity can produce hilarity, and is good to use after activities which require much concentration and effort. Try this with masks, revealing only the eyes.

Questions

How often are you aware what your eyes communicate? Under what circumstances?

Have you ever stared at a stranger? What happened?

Do you like being stared at? Why?

What can you communicate with your eyes?

If you worked with masks, how did it differ?

If you have had someone smile at you with their mouth but not their eyes, how did it make you feel? Why?

What can you read (or think you read) in other people's eyes?

EXPLORING SIZE, RHYTHM, LEVEL, DIRECTION, PACE AND FOCUS

Purpose

To explore ways of varying movement

To see how changing an element changes meaning

To decide what is basic to a movement, and what can vary

To experience how changing an element can evoke new feelings

Participants and Space

Any number, large open space.

Activity

Make up a simple movement pattern that can be repeated easily. (For instance: swing both arms overhead, then collapse.) Repeat the movement until you are sure of it. Make it smaller, larger, faster, slower; use various levels; finally, work with different rhythms. Concentrate on how the variations affect your feelings. Add sounds of different qualities.

Suggestions

Try doing your movement near someone else. Work independently at first, then work off each other. See how the other person affects your work. Relate to people in different ways, in space, with rhythm, on different levels. See how changing one element affects your feelings. (For example, working back to back is different than working face to face; working slowly and with control is different than working with fast, erratic rhythms.)

Questions

Which emotions can be physicalized into movement? Do you think this happens all over the world, or just in our culture?

Why do certain emotions seem to have certain directions and movements (feelings of sadness close you up, and joy opens you)?

Can you tell how people feel from the way they move? Do you think your judgement is accurate?

Can you use these elements to vary paintings, sculpture, music?

How do you decide what element is crucial to the experience, and cannot be changed without altering the experience?

WORKING IN SILENCE

The following activity resulted from a second-grade teacher who felt she was talking too much and not listening enough. She decided to spend an hour in her class without speaking. Her students thought it unfair that she be the only silent one, so they decided no-one could talk. They eliminated sounds, too, because people started grunting and making more noise than they had with speech. The teacher and her students all agreed that the period of total silence helped everybody. It made people pay attention to what was being said non-verbally, and greatly improved concentration. The teacher also felt it provided relaxation, cooled tempers, and refreshed everyone.

Purpose

To gain a different perspective

To work interdependently

To explore non-verbal communication

Participants and Space

Any number, any space.

Activity

Plan an activity for the group, and carry it out without talking or using any sounds to indicate direction or purpose. If possible, do not make the silence the focus of the work; it should be just a way of working.

Suggestions

Work with only the leader silent; then with the group silent. See how long the group can function well without words. Afterward, discuss the effect of silence on the group, the work, and the environment.

Questions

How do you feel when you can not talk?

Do you like working in silence?

How does the silence affect the way the group interacts?

How does it feel to talk after the silence?

How do noises sound after a long period of silence?

How long do you think you could go without talking?

How would you feel if you were mute and unable to talk?

How would this affect the way you functioned in a speaking world?

EXPLORING ACTIONS USING DIFFERENT ATTITUDES

Purpose

To work imaginatively

To learn how attitude affects activity

To explore various attitudes

To work cooperatively

Participants and Space

Start with partners, then include any number; any space.

Activity

Work in pairs. One person initiates an action such as throwing a ball, raking a garden, setting a trap. The partner does the same action, but with a different feeling or attitude. The first person takes on the attitude of the partner, and then starts a new action. Work with various people. Share work with the total group, and discuss problems and possibilities.

Suggestions

The partners could keep the same action, and explore as many different attitudes as possible. They could also start with an attitude, and then do a variety of actions. Work non-verbally but experiment with sounds. Try working with several people at once.

Questions

How does attitude affect action? Does this always hold true?

Can exploring a pretended attitude affect your real attitude? How?

Can you consciously change your real attitude?

Are all people the same to work with? If you have favorites, why?

In daily living, do you see a number of people doing the same action in different ways? What might be the cause of this?

Does an attitude manifest itself in the same way for everyone?

How are attitudes formed? What is the role of environment, physical well-being or sickness, energy, peers?

How do you control your feelings and attitudes?

Have you ever been out of control? What brought you back into control?

COMPLAINING

Some years ago, I worked at a summer camp which had a mixed group of campers. Many of them had never lived in such a primitive setting, and were full of complaints. To avoid building up anger or frustration, the director set aside time after lunch, when the entire camp was assembled, for voicing complaints. There was one stipulation: all complaints had to be *sung*. At first people were very self-conscious, but they soon grew out of this, and began to use the time to full advantage. Singing required more perspective than talking, because the person had to think first of what he/she wanted to say, and how to set it to appropriate music. It not only served to instantly dissipate much anger, and improve conditions where possible; it also uncovered some good voices and sparked campers' interest in writing an operetta about life at the camp.

Purpose

To express one's feelings

To shape the expression of one's feelings

To communicate feelings in unusual ways

Participants and Space

Any number, any space.

Activity

Anyone who has strong negative feelings about conditions that affect most of the group should put their complaints to music, using pre-existing or original melody. People may sing alone or with others, with or without accompaniment. At the time or later, others may reply with a sung response.

Suggestions

If preferred, use poetry, painting or sculpture. Keep a copy of all songs to refer to when looking for ideas. Remember: words must be sung, painted or sculpted; spoken words are not allowed.

Questions

How does the effect of a sung complaint differ from a spoken one?

What effect does having to respond in a similar fashion have?

What do you think of this way of complaining? What other feelings could be expressed this way?

Are there other ways to communicate feelings that would explain and relieve them at the same time?

What effect does shaping your feelings while in the midst of experiencing them have on the feelings?

USING RECYCLED MATERIAL

Much is thrown away by big companies and at home that could be used to great advantage in arts programs. The following are some suggestions for using such materials.

If your class is near a large factory or warehouse, contact the public relations personnel, to find out if anything they discard would be available, or suitable. Sometimes small businesses, such as rug companies, paper manufacturers and material or sewing supply stores, are willing to give ends or seconds at little or no charge.

Plastic bottles can be used as instruments; cut off and made into puppet bodies or heads; cut off to make containers for plants, paints, buttons. They can be cut into odd shapes to use in free-form sculpture. Discovering how odds and ends can be transformed and used creatively is a good activity for people of all ages.

Rolls inside paper products (toilet paper, paper towels, wax paper) are excellent props in improvisation, can be formed into sculptures, or used as instruments. If you can get heavier rolls, such as those used in neoprene (like rubber) or other industrial products, you will find many uses for them. Many games can be devised: one of the favorites is ping-pong toss. Use wide rolls from wrapping paper, and toss and catch the ping-pong ball with the rolls. If people want to have "sword" fights, use rolls; they are easy to obtain, will break before the people do, and still satisfy the need for violence. To get ideas, base an activity on the question: "What can you do with . . . ?"

Odds and ends such as string, ribbon, boxes, packing material, plastic trays, and coffee tins can be collected in a large box, and should be added to continuously. When stimulation is needed, have people go to the box and get a prop.

Once you establish the worth of using that which is generally thrown away, there will be a constant stream of interesting material. One group tried to bring in very strange objects, thinking that they would find something which no-one could use. It never happened.

MAKING MASKS

Purpose

To explore how hiding one's face affects work

To work imaginatively

To use a mask to stimulate improvisation

To explore the grotesque, fantastic and bizarre

Participants and Space

Any number, any space.

Activity

Create a mask that is 3-dimensional, with papier mache, cardboard, or any other material that supports 3-dimensional features. Put on the mask, and assume a body posture that corresponds to the mask. Explore how the new creature would feel, think and act. Exchange masks with other people, trying a variety of masks. Share work with the group, explaining how you worked with a particular mask. Discuss why a mask is easy or difficult, in terms of comfort and ideas. Working with one or two others, create a group improvisation based on characters from specific masks. Use pieces of material or props that help to define the character further.

Suggestions

Look for props that help stimulate the imagination, such as canes, sticks, hats, belts, and gloves. Try masks that cover the whole face and masks that leave the jaw free. Use words and/or sounds. Paint the way the new character makes you feel. Write a description of how your character lives, with whom, and what it does. Think how your character would act in different cultures at different times (early Greek, Restoration).

Questions

What effect does changing the place or time have on the character?

How does a prop affect the character?

How does it feel to wear a mask, and not use your own face?

How does wearing a mask affect your perception?

How does wearing a mask affect speech and movement?

ADD A LINE (STORY, PICTURE, SONG)

Purpose

To develop imagination

To develop confidence in sharing ideas

To develop stories cooperatively

To discover which stories work best as drama or painting

Participants and Space

Any number; groups of 6 or 8 to start; any space.

Activity

Have each person contribute one sentence to a story, one line to a drawing, or one phrase to a song until everyone has contributed and/or the work is finished. Work from a prearranged theme or subject if desired. If the group is working on a story, let each person paint a response to it; if it is doing a painting, act out a response. If the group has been writing a song, establish a context for it.

Suggestions

The quality of work in this activity improves with practice. Making connections between art and music, words and color, and music and place reveal how feelings, ideas and attitudes can be expressed. Some ideas are expressed more clearly in song than in speech; some feelings are better expressed in movement than in painting.

Questions

How do you feel when it is your turn to contribute?

How important is the work that has preceded yours?

How do you get started?

How do you use the material you are presented with?

What serves as creative stimulus for your stories, pictures, or songs?

WORKING ON AND OFF CENTER AS A GROUP

Purpose

To experience how individual stability can become group stability

To experience sharing center

To work cooperatively, with control

Participants and Space

Any number, large open space.

Small children will have some difficulty with this activity, so work with a few at a time, slowly.

Activity

Divide into groups of five or six. Work off center by yourself. On prearranged signal, lean slightly against a person near you until everyone in the group is leaning against someone else, while continuing to move in place. The group should thus be supporting each other so individual instability becomes group stability. This is sharing center. Find your own center again, and repeat the activity, losing your center in a different way. Add sound as appropriate.

Suggestions

Work with different levels, degrees of energy, dynamics and body parts. Try not using your arms to find new possibilities. Create improvisational situations that would call for this response. Work with people of different size and weight. Move around the room off-center, and come together to create on-center movement.

Questions

How do you feel when sharing center?

How do you develop trust in the group not to drop you?

Are there parallels to this activity in daily living?

What effect does changing levels, dynamics, pace or focus have on your feelings while you are working?

How do you feel toward your group after this activity?

Are there some groups that have difficulty sharing center? If so, why? How could this situation be improved?

What effect does working to different kinds of music have?

YARN PICTURES

Purpose

To use yarn to make pictures

To work cooperatively and imaginatively

To explore and enjoy the process of creating, as much as the finished product

Participants and Space

Any number, any space; working on a rug helps keep the yarn from slipping.

Activity

Each person should have some lengths of yarn, one to two feet long, in various colors and textures. It is best to work in groups of three, though two or four are also possible. One person puts down his/her piece of yarn, any way desired. The second person puts his/her yarn down, changing or adding to what has been done. Each person continues to add another piece of yarn until the group feels that the work is completed. This should be done non-verbally. When finished, the groups should discuss among themselves what they think of their work. Share all work.

Suggestions

Try discussing how the picture makes you feel, or what you were thinking about while adding a particular piece of yarn.

Encourage people to use a lot of space, to make big pictures, since there is a tendency to work small. Some groups get very attached to their work and want to save it. This can be done by slipping paper under the yarn and setting it with spray-starch. The thought that each piece of yarn can make many pictures, however, usually convinces people that every work does not have to be saved. Mix the groups, so various combinations of people get a chance to work together.

Questions

Does it bother you not to save your work?

Do you enjoy the process of doing something enough not to care if the finished product is seen only by you or your group and then disassembled?

What kinds of finished work should be preserved? Who decides?

Are some people easier to work with than others? Why?

Are some yarns more stimulating than others? Which, and why?

How do groups you have worked with differ? How are they similar?

What kinds of feelings can you express using yarn? Are there some you could not express?

USING STRING TO CREATE STORIES

Purpose

To explore how line and shape evoke feelings

To work with color and line uninhibitedly

To explore how one experience can create another

Participants and Space

Any number, any space in which there is room to move.

Activity

Each person should have a length of heavy string or twine, about four feet long. Place the string on a large piece of paper, or on several pieces of shirt cardboard stapled together. When satisfied with the shape of the string, place a sheet of paper over it, and secure it with tape or paper clips. Using crayons, rub the lines until you have an imprint of the string design on the paper below. Remove the tape and use the paper with the rubbed design for the next phase of the work. (Save the string and cardboard.)

Hang up all rubbings, and have each person pick a design to work with. The person should then move the way the design makes him/her feel. Decide who might move that way, and what the person might be doing. When each person is ready, combine three or four people, and have them create a group story that can be shared with the total group. Work with several designs and different people, to explore several possibilities.

Suggestions

Leave the rubbing designs up for a few days, or try working with them after some time, to explore the effect time has on the work. Combine several designs into one. Work with color, looking for the effect it has on feelings or ideas.

Questions

Can you use string to create a design based on a particular feeling?

Can you change the feeling by using a different color?

Can you identify or sense feelings in the work of others?

How can you use line to inspire movement?

Do you use different parts of your body, or rely mostly on arms?

What would happen if you structured movement around various levels and strange positions?

What effect does the passage of time have on your work and your response to the work of others?

USING A STILL CAMERA (I)

Purpose

To develop perspective

To sharpen observation powers

To look at ordinary events with a fresh eye

Participants and Space

Any number, any space, but preferably one in which there is a variety of objects and people

Activity

Using a still camera, take pictures of people or objects that are interesting. Do not look only for pretty surfaces; look for interesting feelings, actions, relationships. Keep a record of what you are shooting, and why. Seeing the developed photograph may blur your memory and your original response.

Suggestions

Share photographs with a partner, and then with the larger group. Compare your own response and that of others. Discuss how different people view the same thing differently, and how this gives rise to various opinions. Describe to others what you see in a particular photograph, what is significant, and your emotional response.

Questions

How does working in black and white differ from color? Are there times when one is more or less effective?

What types of people or objects catch your eye?

What do you look for in subject matter?

How does the presence of the photographer qualify taking the picture and response of the subject? Can it be changed?

How does taking someone else's picture compare with having someone take a picture of you?

How does using a camera affect your ability to see?

What do you learn about another person by looking at his/her photographs?

What insights do you gain by looking at your own photographs?

USING A STILL CAMERA (II)

Purpose

To explore the effect of mood on photography

To use film imaginatively

To use photographs communicatively

Participants and Space

Any number, any space; preferably an interesting environment.

Activity

Starting with a specific mood (real or imagined), take photographs that reflect and explore that mood. Work either abstractly or narratively and objectively. Use both black & white and color film. When developed, arrange them in a way that expresses the mood. Share the finished arrangements with partners and then with the group. Try using a single picture on a common theme to create a group response.

Suggestions

If you have access to an enlarger, experiment with various sizes of each picture. Also experiment with the shape of the picture. Try various compositions, both within any one picture, and combining several pictures. Create a group collage, using a theme or not. The collage can include paintings, drawings, three-dimensional sculpture. Choose an appropriate musical accompaniment. Write stories based on the work.

Questions

How do you select a visual image that will express a mood?

What are the differences in the subjects people choose? What are the similarities?

Can you evoke the same emotions in a viewer of a finished photograph that you felt when taking it?

How does size affect a photograph?

What effect does color have?

Have you ever experienced a photograph blown up to room-sized proportions? How does it make you feel?

What is the difference in your response to a painting and to a photograph of the same subject?

What is the effect of the environment on your picture-taking, factors such as sounds, smells, lighting, external pressures?

How does cultural conditioning affect the taking and viewing of pictures?

USING A MOVIE CAMERA

Purpose

To explore motion

To explore how observation changes, using a motion rather than a still camera

To explore the effect of editing

Participants and Space

Any number; space depends on the subject to be filmed.

Activity

Divide into small groups of three or four, each with their own movie camera. Choose a mood, story or situation which everyone will use; send each group out to shoot a film. Share rushes, and the edited film, recording comments from both stages. Experiment with records, tapes or live sounds to make a sound track. If possible, have a few groups use color film.

Suggestions

You can also work without a pre-determined theme or subject, although a common theme shows clearly how differently people respond to the same thing. Try projecting silent films on all four walls of a room at the same time, so the group is surrounded by simultaneous motion pictures. Try filming the same experience at different times and under different circumstances.

Questions

How do your moods influence your work?

What effect does sound have on a visual experience?

How does motion affect emotional response?

How significant a role can editing play?

How would each film have differed if there had been different people in each group, or if each person had shot his/her own film?

What effect does color have on the finished product?

USING OLD FILMS

Purpose

To create new films from old

To create motion environments and explore their effect on feelings

To work cooperatively

To experiment with color, pattern, and images

Participants and Space

Small groups with five and six people; space to project films.

Activity

Each group should have a length of old film. Using Clorox, or a similar product, bleach the film. Sometimes, leave parts of the film unbleached for a particular effect. Run the bleached film under cold water and let it dry. When dry, use magic markers and create new shapes and colors on the film. When finished, have the groups project their films to see if they achieved the desired effect. Then have each group tape an accompanying sound track. Share all films.

Using your own, or another group's film, respond to it in movement. From memory, making up poems or stories, verbalize how the film made you feel. Share responses with the group. Work with various films to see how the experience changes.

Suggestions

Select an old film with action you would like to use. One group used an old newsreel of a ship sinking, keeping part of the sound track too. Obtain films from newspaper advertisements, film supply houses, movie-makers, and schools that have old films to throw away. Time needed to make a film depends on the age and experience of the group. Divide this activity into three sessions, to avoid making any session too long. Try projecting several films at once, or on all four walls, if you can get enough projectors.

Questions

How does designing on film differ from designing on paper?
How do you feel responding to your own work?
Do the films affect your feelings? Can they change your mood?
How does it feel to watch several films simultaneously?
Can you watch this type of film without trying to figure out what it is, or what the creators were trying to do?

Can the films create new environments to stimulate you?
Do films give you many new ideas?

USING COLOR TO STIMULATE RESPONSE
Purpose
To explore the effect of color on the individual
To discover how color can affect mood
To see how color can affect spatial perception
To work cooperatively and imaginatively
Participants and Space
Any number that space and supplies can serve.
Activity
Create structures out of cardboard boxes, wire, or a tent. Line the inside with panels of colored paper so the whole interior is one color. Each structure should be a different color. Everyone should help create a structure, so the number of structures depends on the number of people.

Go inside the structure in groups of three or four, and experience the color. If images come to mind, share them; also share feelings. One person might record these images and feelings. Each group in turn should experience at least three different colors.

Working in small groups, create a movement piece, poem, short story or drama, based on the way the color made you feel. Share work with the total group.

Suggestions

Think out the size and shape of the structure carefully, so the exterior as well as the interior is interesting. Put a different color on the outside, and see what the effect is on the perception of the color inside. Discuss how color affects each person, seeing which colors elicit similar or different responses, and what stimulation they provide. Try this activity with pools of light; red and purple are very effective.

Questions

Are you aware of the effects that colors have on you?

Do you have favorite colors? Do you know why you like them and dislike others?

Do you choose clothes or food because of color?

Do you think most people respond the same way to the same color? Why or why not?

If you could change the color scheme of your home, school or office, what colors would you choose? Why?

USING SMELLS (I)

Purpose

To become aware of the effect of smells on feelings and ideas

To use smell to stimulate the imagination

To work imaginatively

To explore what makes a person feel a certain way toward a particular smell

To explore the effect of smell on memory

Participants and Space

Any number; space in which there is room to move.

Activity

Have each person bring in a smell. (It must be isolated and contained, so the room is not filled with different smells.) Working with a partner, experience the smell without looking at the source. Describe how the smell makes you feel, what it brings to mind, if it were smelled before, and what the occasion was.

Then think of a story stimulated by the smell. When you finish, reverse roles with your partner. If possible, pass the smells around, so everyone can work with different smells. It is good to do this outdoors, if weather and space permit.

Questions

Are there smells you definitely do or do not like? What are they, and why?

What effect does the smell of a person or place have on the way you feel about them?

Does an awful smell ever become a good smell or vice-versa? What causes the change?

If blindfolded, could you identify where you were by its smell?

Could you identify someone you know by smell?

Do people from different cultures smell different? How and why?

What are your feelings about working with, and talking about, smell?

Does our culture influence our feelings about smell?

USING TEXTURE

Purpose

To become aware of texture

To stimulate the imagination

To work cooperatively

To see texture as an environmental factor

Participants and Space

As many people as can comfortably use the space available.

Activity

Before working, have each person select three items with an interesting texture, and put them in separate paper bags. When the group meets, put all bags in the center of the space. Each person selects a bag and, without looking at the contents, feels what is inside. Consider what the textures make you think of, how they affect feelings (cold cooked spaghetti feels squishy, like worms), and if they repel or attract.

Select one or all of the feelings and images evoked by encountering the textures, and explore them using movement, song, drama, clay, crayon, paints, or other media. If the feeling from the texture begins to fade, return to the bag. When ready, share work, but still without having looked at the contents of the bag. If there is time, try other bags. This can be done individually, with partners, in groups. When the texture ceases to be a source of stimulation, look at the contents of the bag.

Suggestions

Before bringing in bags, discuss different types of texture, and

look at and feel various textures in the room. After completing the activity, discuss which textures felt good, bad, or whatever.

Questions

Does temperature affect texture?

Are you aware of textures in daily living?

What part does texture play in interior decoration and architecture?

How did you select items for the paper bags?

Were there items you wanted to use that would not fit in the bag or that might have spoiled? If so, what were they?

USING FOUND OBJECTS (I)

Purpose

To use ordinary objects in an extraordinary way

To explore fantasy individually and as a group

To work cooperatively

To become conscious of the environment

Participants and Space

As many people as move comfortably in the available space.

Activity

Have each person bring an object and explore what it could become. (A chair can become a motorcycle, a horse, a gun.) Find a way of showing how you would use it, rather than describing how it could be used. Try adding sounds. Work with a partner and combine your ideas. Share work with the total group. Work in threes or fours, exploring a variety of ideas in the creation of a larger group work. When sharing work with the total group, have the group sit in different configurations: circle, semi-circle, straight in front, different levels. Share differences in perception.

Suggestions

If space is limited, find out how much space people need to work in without hurting each other. It is fine to swing chairs in a gym, but dangerous in a small room. Make sure people select objects that are light and easily handled, and that will not cause strain. Small children sometimes try to pick up tables to use as capes. When sharing work, stress the multiplicity of ideas, giving imagination free rein.

Questions

How did you decide what an object could be?

How did you have to modify your ideas when working in pairs, or in small groups?

What is the essence of an idea?

How do you decide what is central to an idea and what can be modified or varied?

USING FOUND OBJECTS (II)

Purpose

To use objects to stimulate the imagination

To shift emphasis from what something is, to how to use it

To work cooperatively

To become conscious of the environment

To be aware of texture, color, shape and sound

To explore fantasy individually and as a group

Participants and Space

As many people as can move comfortably in the space available.

Activity

Find objects such as boxes, packing material, industrial surplus, that are without sharp edges and unbreakable. (Note: many local industries welcome requests for surplus materials or items to be thrown away.) There should be enough objects to permit each member to work individually. Find a way of using the object that is not based on what it "really" is. Let the object suggest an environment, a feeling, a fantasy. For example, a cardboard box would be a dangerous environment if it collapses while walking on it. When everybody has some ideas, share the work, placing the emphasis on opening up ideas, rather than judging some good and some bad.

Work with a partner and combine ideas. The sharing often results in a totally new idea. Use sounds and gibberish as well as words. Share the new work, see what ideas your work gives to others.

Divide into small groups. Select the object(s) you would like to work with. Have each group create a piece based on the stimulus of the object. Share work with others.

Suggestions

If you are unable to think of anything, try moving with the object. Ask questions starting with, "What would happen if . . ." Often, the problem is that people censor ideas before trying them. Think of multiple uses for an object. For example, one group turned some foam stripping into a fire hose, a magic path, and a magical snake that granted wishes. The most difficult part is to overcome embarrassment, self-consciousness, and the feeling that one's ideas are "stupid." Encouraging fantasy and non-judgemental reception helps make future work richer and more exciting.

Questions

Are you more concerned with what something *is* than with what it might become?

How can you use your senses to get ideas not based on actual
use? How do you feel working this way?

Is it more fun to work with a group?

What do you see, hear or feel about other people's work that
gives you new ideas?

SOUND STORIES (I)

Purpose

To use sounds to stimulate ideas

To become more aware of sound

To work imaginatively with sound

To work cooperatively

Participants and Space

Partners and small groups, with space in which to move.

Activity

Find a sound that is pleasing or interesting to you. It can be a
body sound (hitting your thigh with your hand), a musical
sound (hitting bottles filled with different levels of water), or a
percussive sound (hitting a box). Avoid conventional musical
instruments, however, since this forces people to listen more
closely to other sounds, and become aware of other
possibilities. Work in pairs first, with one making the sound
while the other listens with eyes closed. The listener should tell
the sound-maker what images come to mind, and what activities could follow the sound. Then reverse roles, giving both
partners a chance to listen and to make sounds.

As time and interest permit, new partners should form to experience new sounds. Groups of four can work, with two play-

ing and two listening. Listeners can respond together, creating ensembles rather than solos. Try to use the sound as the end of a story as well as the beginning.

Suggestions

Tape the sound ahead of time, so nobody knows what produces it. Discourage people from guessing the source of the sound. Encourage thinking about what it could or could not be. If sound isolation is a problem, make the sound under blankets or in a box.

Questions

Does it bother you *not* to be asked to identify the sound?

Do you feel comfortable responding to the way sounds make you feel?

Can you find a place where there is absolutely no sound?

How many sounds can you hear at one time?

What sound level do you prefer?

Do you ever crave quiet?

What, to you, is the difference between sound and noise?

USING GROUP PAINTING AND PUPPETRY

Most work done in schools and in jobs involves individual response. There are few chances for people to work in groups, and cooperate as teams. Pick-up games (in which anyone who is around can play) have given way to Little League, Scouts, and other organized activity. Order is imposed externally, by referees, officials, and in the case of children, by parents. People give up team sports in their twenties, and games tend to become individualized. There is little if any time or place for a group to work or play together, making its own rules and developing its way of solving problems. Considering the large number of teenagers and adults who feel isolated one factor might be the absence of such team activities. Working with a group not only has salutary effects; its absence can also be harmful.

Painting a group picture does not solve the problem of alienation in modern society. It does, however, provide people with a good way of working together, especially when members of the group do not get along. It seems incredible, but one of the reasons people in a group do not cooperate is that they often simply *do not know how*. The following is a good example of group painting.

Recently, a 4th-grade teacher was so upset by a group of students who continually disrupted her art class that she was ready to ask the principal to give them to some other teacher. She decided to investigate the kind of experience the children had in the class preceding hers, and discovered that they came from a teacher who demanded absolute silence and immobility.

Realizing that the children were reacting to this repression, she looked for a way to allow them to express their feelings with a minimum of violence, noise, and disorder.

The next time her class met, she told the children to remove their shoes at the door. This caught them off their guard enough to let her explain that they were going to paint the way they felt on the paper she had taped all over the floor (she had moved desks and chairs out of the way). Each child put on a painting smock, and then began to paint furiously. Some paint was spilled, some was thrown, but most reached the paper. When there was no space left, the teacher asked the children how they felt about the work. They said they were too close to it, so the teacher suggested they hang it up outside. The children were impressed that she would display their work, since they had sensed her dissatisfaction with their work previously. The period was almost over, so the work was not discussed until the next class meeting.

In this class, several students discussed problems openly. They admitted they had disliked coming to art class, but they also said that they wanted to do another painting. After doing a few more paintings, which the teacher hung up, she asked them to look at all their work, and respond to that using paint, charcoal, crayon or clay. When this was done, the group sat in a circle on the floor and spoke at length about what they felt had happened. Discipline was no longer a problem. The children were now eager to work, and had to be forced to leave. When asked for explanations, the children spoke of the difficulty in going from one teacher who gave them no freedom to another who gave them a great deal; it was hard to sit still in an art class after having been still for so long. They had been unable to contain explosive feelings, and felt that they needed to have a chance to move around before having to concentrate on the art work. Many children commented that the first paintings they had done were very wild compared to the later ones. They also noticed that, in the response work, many paintings revealed chaos becoming order, scribble becoming articulated line, muddied colors becoming clear and controlled.

There are no panaceas. If you scold someone for not paying attention, you may exacerbate rather than solve the problem. It is often more helpful to give the person or group the chance to express their feelings in a safe way, without fear of punishment or judgement. Expressing and analyzing feelings gives people a chance to see alternative ways of responding, letting them choose their behavior rather than being victimized by it.

Another teacher, working with older people who were very angry but inarticulate, found that the group responded to the idea of making puppets. The instructions were to make the puppets as grotesque as possible. The person who had caused them much anger and frustration had a big nose; the nose on the one-foot puppet they made was six inches long. In creating the puppet show, the group saw how they wanted to handle the situation in real life. The show became a kind of social role-playing, which permitted the students to explore alternatives in safety. Knocking a puppet's head off is much less dangerous than knocking off a person's head, yet a similar kind of energy is released.

USING COLOR AND LINE

People in our culture often feel they cannot draw or paint. This becomes more true as the person grows older. Yet painting is a marvelous way to externalize and express feelings, especially when the paper covers the width or length of the room. Working together on an enormous piece of paper, people are often able to lose inhibitions.

Purpose

To use color and line to express feelings

To work imaginatively and with cooperation

To be sensitive to the effect of color on feelings

To use line rhythmically and joyfully

Participants and Space

Any number, depending on material and space available.

Activity

Cover the floor and/or walls with paper. Working from a predetermined stimulus (an incident, story, poem, image), to music, or just spontaneously, have each person paint how he/she feels. It is good to have fairly thick brushes, vibrant colors, and enough space so people do not bump into each other. People should feel free to paint as they please, and for as long as they please. There should be no attempt to fill up the papered area; nor is it necessary to have a unifying color scheme. When everyone has finished, the group should look at the total work, comment or not, and reflect on how the work makes them feel. If possible, hang the work in a place where it is easily seen, so the painters have a chance to look at their work over a period of time.

Suggestions

Have people work barefoot, and try painting with the toes. Use the work to stimulate poems, stories, songs, sculpture. If several groups have done this, exchange work, using the new work as stimulus for a new experience.

Questions

How does this experience differ from an individual drawing assignment that is specific and directed?

How do you feel when you are finished, compared with when you started?

How do you feel using your toes to paint with? How else would you like to try painting?

What is the difference painting to different kinds of music?

USING PAPER

Purpose

To work imaginatively

To explore how paper can be used to express emotions

To use paper to create costumes, settings, and environments

To show what can be done with inexpensive, readily available material

Participants and Space

Any number, large space with high ceilings if possible.

Activity

Paper can be used in an infinite variety of ways. You can roll up newspaper to make swords (you lose when your roll is bent); you can tear it into tiny bits to make a snowstorm; you can cut and shape it to make costumes, fold it to make hats, props, even furniture. Paper towers are fun to knock over; sounds can be made from paper-based percussive instruments. You can transform a room using paper decorations. One group created a prison environment by filling the room with paper walls which "guards" pretended to electrify. Prisoners fashioned a paper tunnel for their escape, using paper guns.

Suggestions

Paper is a good material to work with because it is readily available in huge amounts at no cost. A paper sword is safe, and the variety of paper hats which can be made provide endless ways to costume characters. Have groups work together to create sculptures, environments, instruments for a group percussion orchestra, and so on.

Questions

What properties of paper give you ideas?

How can you use paper to help express how you feel?

What ways can you use paper to relieve anger?

How could you use paper if you felt lonely?

Using only paper, could you make a mountain that could be climbed?

How would you feel in a room all filled with paper? What could you do with it all?

MOVING SHAPES TO CREATE CHARACTERS

Purpose

To stimulate the imagination

To work cooperatively

To create situations from character interaction

To respond spontaneously to newly created situations

To develop kinesthetic sense memory

Participants and Space

Any number, fairly large space.

Young children will need help getting started. They will understand more quickly if you create animals rather than people.

Older people who feel they are not creative may respond more quickly to what the character is *doing*, rather than who the character *is*.

Activity

Have one person spin around and stop on command. Have the group look at the position of the person, and consider the kind of person it might be, what the person might be doing, where the person might be going. Each person should remember his/her position, so it can be re-assumed later.

When everybody's position has been discussed, have people assume the original positions and interact with each other, as particular characters. A predetermined time or place can unify the activity (a carnival, marketplace, forest, factory). The leader may add more qualifications: a storm is coming.

Suggestions

Having the group suggest what the person might be takes pressure off people who have trouble finding ideas. If the group offers more than one solution, the individual should choose one. There is no need to rush on to the interactions; spend as long as necessary on the speculations. If people feel uncomfortable after a few tries, have them draw from a box full of hats, clothes, objects or props to stimulate the imagination. It may help to give characters names.

Questions

What kinds of cues do you use to infer qualities of character from the position of the body?

Can the same position suggest different types of qualities?

What effect does giving a character a name have on the character?

How do you remember your own shape?

USING FOOD (I)

Purpose

To become aware of the effects of taste, texture and smell

To see how one judges food by the way it looks

To explore how eating stimulates memory

To work imaginatively

Participants and Space

Any number, any space in which there is room to move.

Young children should do this after lunch, to avoid chaos.

Check beforehand to see if there are any food allergies before doing this.

Activity

Have each person bring in some food (enough for three people to taste), that is in a plain wrapper, so the food cannot be seen. Work with foods that the group is not familiar with. Work in partners, with one person feeding the other, without letting the eater see or smell the food. The eater should tell what the food makes him/her feel or think about. Repeat, letting the eater see the food, and then share the new response. Reverse roles. Try the activity with new people, so each is fed and feeds at least three others. Share feelings about the experience with the total group.

Suggestions

Before meeting, discuss food that should and should not be brought in. If the leader does not have a good rapport with the group, this activity should not be attempted, to avoid eating spoiled or inedible things. Reject any kind of pills or medicine. Help people explore how they feel about being fed something they cannot see or smell, and how food affects memory.

Questions

What associations do certain foods have for you? Why?

How do you feel being fed? Especially something you cannot see or smell?

Do you react negatively to certain foods before you eat them? Why?

How do your, and other people's, reactions differ to the same food?

What kind of experiences shape your reaction to food?

What makes one person willing to try anything, and another unwilling?

Are you adventurous in experimenting with new foods? Do you try to taste foods from other countries?

What makes you decide you like or dislike a particular food?

WORKING IN SOMEONE ELSE'S SPACE (I)

Purpose

To develop spatial awareness

To experience how pace affects perception

To work with concentration

To work cooperatively

Participants and Space

Any number, any space.

Young children will find this more difficult than older people.

Activity

Have two people face each other. Each person moves his/her arms in the open spaces. (One arm can go in the space created by partner's arm being away from the body, or overhead.) Both partners should work at the same time, trying to avoid touching each other. Use as many levels as possible (between legs, over the head). As competence increases, work with more speed. Change partners, and use other parts of the body.

Suggestions

Work in groups of 3 or 4. Try different levels of tension, with varying levels of sound. It is difficult to combine harsh sound and gentle movement. People with perceptual problems should work individually, finding space slowly.

Questions

What do you do if a space you thought was empty becomes filled as you are moving toward it?

Can you predict accurately your partner's movement, and the direction of the movement?

What cues do you receive? How can they be made more or less obvious?

What does working faster do to your perception? What adjustments do you make for increased speed?

What effect does sound (made by you or others) have on your work?

How do you feel about working so closely with another person?

ESTABLISHING IDENTITY (I)
Purpose
To become sensitive to cues revealing who and what a person is and does

To learn what kind of non-verbal signals a person gives to others

To explore how relationships affect people

Participants and Space

Any number of people in the group, working with partners, any space.

Activity

One of the partners decides on an identity to assume. In the beginning, to simplify things, be a member of the family: a grandfather, a grandchild. Through action and words, the first person should make it clear what his/her identity is. When this is established, change roles. When everyone has had a chance, discuss how the identity was established. After some experience, try possibilities outside the family relationships.

Suggestions

Have one pair, who know who they are, work in the center of the group. Have the rest of the group determine their identities. Decide who they could and could not be, and why. Suggest ways they might, and would never, behave.

Questions

What cues do you use to decide who a person is? Are these cues always accurate?

In daily living, have you ever thought you knew who a person was, and later discovered you were wrong?

What cues gave you the wrong information, making the wrong decision?

Have you ever consciously decided to give other people the wrong information about yourself, verbally or nonverbally? How long did this wrong impression last?

PERSONAL DRAMA

There is great value in sharing exciting events and emotions, especially in a non-judgemental, supportive environment. In general, young children and inexperienced students should work with fewer elements. With experience, even young children can re-enact complicated emotional experiences. Sometimes one role can be so unappealing to the group that nobody wants to play it. The following are examples of sharing experiences through drama.

Some fourth grade girls from a very poor, low-level reading group were participating in a dramatic project whose theme was Cinderella. Nobody wanted to play the two ugly sisters or the step-mother. After a long time, one girl asked, "Could the reason the sisters and step-mother were so ugly be that nobody loved them, and they didn't know any better? Maybe when Cinderella is loved by the Prince, she can love her sisters and step-mother. Then they will stop being ugly and will find husbands to love them."

This was a satisfactory explanation, and soon three children volunteered to be the sisters and the step-mother. Knowing that the ugliness would not last, they made themselves as ugly and miserable as they could. This gave them a chance to think about what happens to people who do not feel loved or wanted, an experience they were all familiar with.

They developed their own script, costumes and set (the group painted a huge mural), and then decided that they wanted to share their work with others. They presented their play to two other schools, and had part of it shown on a local television station. The girls decided they liked their own version better than the original, and wrote out the script with the help of the teacher, illustrated and bound it, and put it in the school library in the collection of children's plays.

Another time, a group of first graders were recounting personal incidents to the class. One child told how she had thrown a ball to her dog. The ball rolled into the street, the dog ran after it, and the dog was hit by a fast moving car. No-one wanted to play the child who threw the ball. The girl kept saying, "I didn't mean to kill my dog, I loved my dog." Since the child was close to tears, something had to be done to help the other children understand how she felt. The leader asked how many people could hit a wall with a ball. Almost everyone raised their hands. The leader then drew a circle on the wall, and gave each child a chance to hit it with the ball. Only two hit the circle. When asked why they had not gotten the ball in the circle, they all said that they had tried, and had not meant to miss. The leader then reminded them that the girl had not meant to throw the ball into the street. After a short silence one child remarked, "It must feel terrible to think you're playing with your dog and then watch him killed. You must have felt awful." When the drama was re-enacted, each child wanted to have a turn playing the girl with the ball. After the dog was hit, all of the children would say, "Don't worry, you didn't mean to kill your dog, it was an accident."

In both these examples, a non-judgemental view of the behavior was needed. Once the children understood that the ugly people were not ugly because they wanted to be, and that the child had not purposely killed the dog, the dramas could be re-enacted, and served as exercises in understanding and compassion.

Older people are more reluctant to act out personal dramas. A good way to get them started is to have them give examples of common scenes that recur in nightmares, such as: being chased, falling, drowning, being unjustly accused, or screaming without being heard. The following activity works well with older people.

Purpose
> To share meaningful personal experiences
> To understand other people's feelings
> To respond comfortably to emotional situations
> To respond open-mindedly, without passing judgement

Participants and Space
> Any number, with space for all groups to work.
> Young children should start in groups of three or four, with a leader.
> Older children and adults can start with groups of four or five, but if they are uncomfortable, have the whole group act out one event.

Activity
> Have one person relate something that happened; a real incident, a dream or a fantasy. In the beginning, use a simple story,

such as: "I went to the ocean to swim, but the current was so strong it pulled me back and I almost drowned." One person can play the swimmer, and everyone else the ocean (break it down into waves, sounds, rocks, sea life). When the group feels confortable, divide into smaller groups and share experiences until each group finds one they want to work with. Give each person a chance to have his/her drama enacted. It helps if the person whose story is used does *not* play him/herself.

Suggestions

When the group acts as a whole, explore variations that enhance, but do not change, the story. For example: suppose there were two swimmers instead of one; one is a good swimmer, the other is not. Suppose it is the good swimmer who gets in trouble. Suppose a storm develops; see how the sounds, rhythms and movements change. Create the scene before the swimmers enter the water: are they on an empty or crowded beach? Did anyone warn them? Do they speak the same language as the people on the beach? Also enact the aftermath.

Begin your questions with, "What would happen if" (older instead of younger, sick instead of well, and so on). It is important when working with personal drama to provide group discussions but to exclude comments of liking or disliking. At this stage, judgements are irrelevant. The purpose of this and similar activities is to explore feelings, not to create finished theatre pieces.

Questions

What kinds of experiences are easy to share?

What experiences are difficult to share?

How do you feel telling a personal experience to a group?

Do you prefer working with a large or small group?

Can you explore different points of view without judging whether they are good or bad?

How do groups differ?

Are there some people in some groups that make it harder or easier to relate an experience? Why?

How do you feel when someone relates an experience which is similar to one that you have been through?

Is it difficult for you to relive someone else's experience?

How do you imagine a response to something you have never experienced?

How do you feel toward the group after this kind of work? Toward yourself?

Do you sense a difference in the way people work after doing this kind of activity for a while? If so, what is the difference?

USING STAGE COMBAT TECHNIQUES

Because violence is such a pervasive influence in everyone's lives, and is so dramatic, it is often used to solve problems, in both real life and improvisational work. Although alternatives should be stressed, most people enjoy the power they feel when a faked punch is thrown, and the opponent is knocked to the floor. Many improvisations can be developed using stage combat, which will use excess tension and energy, help focus attention on a partner, and provide an excellent vicarious experience for people (timid and aggressive) who are afraid of exploring violent situations.

To learn how to stage fights, consult the following books: *Stage Fight: Swords, firearms, fisticuffs and slapstick*, by William Hobbs, published by Theatre Arts, New York, 1967; and *Sword and Masque*, by Julius Palffy-Alpar, published by F.A. Davis & Co., Philadelphia, 1967.

It is important to remember that, no matter how experienced people may be, always start to practice a staged fight in slow motion, and increase the tempo gradually. If the group has trouble maintaining the slow tempo, beat out a pulse on a drum or have the class keep time clapping.

MASSAGE
Purpose
   To relax body tension
   To become aware of the physical manifestations of tension
   To work cooperatively
Participants and Space
   Partners; space in which to work without disturbing others
Activity
   Excessive tension, caused by physical or emotional activity, makes muscles hard, rigid and often painful. Discussing problems has little effect on the muscles. There are books on massage which go into greater detail than is possible for this book; two of the good ones available are: *The Massage Book*

by George Downing (New York: Random House, 1972) and *Book of Massage* by Gunilla Knutson (New York: St. Martin's Press, 1972). It is helpful to know some general principles, however, so this activity will show you how to begin.

The chief areas to consider are: the face, soles of the feet, the shoulders, neck and back, the arms and fingers. Most of these areas can be self-massaged. In general, strokes should be smooth, circular and firm. Once the hands are in contact with the body, they should remain there until the massage is finished. The best position is lying on a massage table, but these are seldom available. The next best is to have the person lie on the floor on a mat or blanket. Massages can also be given, however, when the person to be massaged is sitting, standing or leaning. Usually the pads of the thumbs are used, while the rest of the fingers support.

Suggestions

Have all the people in the room form a circle, with each person massaging the neck and shoulders of the person in front. After a while, change direction, so each person gets rubbed by a different person. Adjust differences in height by changing places or using stools.

Have the group work in pairs, sitting, facing each other. At the same time, each rubs the other's temples, cheeks, neck and head, adjusting pressure according to partner's desire. Massage the fleshy and not the bony areas of the body. Tiny lumps of tension can be eased by massage, but the novice should avoid sores, injuries and very painful areas.

To massage the feet, remove socks, support the rest of the foot, and make the person comfortable. Often a great deal of fatigue can be relived by massaging the balls of the feet, toes, and calves.

Work with firm strokes, checking with your partner to adjust pressure. Massaging with your eyes closed sometimes increases your ability to feel tension in your partner.

Stroke more firmly when working toward the heart, less firmly as you move away. This imitates the breath cycle of active inhalation, passive exhalation. The person giving the massage should work with ease and personal relaxation.

Questions

Can you see any change in the shape of the muscles before and after massage?

Does massage make you feel less tired?

Does a massage give you more energy?

How do you feel when you are being massaged?

Do you like to give massages?

Is there a difference in the way people feel and act toward each other after massage?

SECTION III

The activities in this final section require good group rapport, emotional freedom, and confidence in reacting spontaneously. Each person should work with self-discipline and self-motivation. Teachers should encourage students to make up their own activities, using the suggestions in this book as a point of reference or departure. It is not necessary to try all of the activities before making up their own.

By now, students and teachers should have developed a basis on which to develop judgement. The emphasis should be on establishing criteria which are based on respect for the effort. Students should be comfortable describing what they do and do not see, and why it is significant. Continue to stress the development of work, not the production of finished pieces. Critical judgement, careful observation and precise description must all be practiced before the pressure of performance is added.

Many exciting plays, sound stories, sculptures and paintings will result from this level of work, and people will be tempted to perform for others. It is important to remember who the work is for, and why, in order to prevent the work from being compromised for audience approval.

One group, for instance, developed a very powerful play about life on their streets, which included cursing, prostitution and drug-related violence. The children wanted to perform it for their parents but the principal would permit it only if they "cleaned it up." Resentfully, they agreed, though when their teacher asked them *why* they thought it should be "cleaned up," they had no answer. In discussing it with their teacher, they began to understand what the effect on their play would be if it were changed in accordance with the principal's wishes. They decided that either the work would be shown as is, or not at all. Many parents had heard about the play, and wanted to see it performed, so they arranged for a production in a nearby church. By refusing to submit to an unreasonable order, the children learned to stand up for their rights of self-expression, and of artistic and moral freedom.

USING SMELLS (II)

Purpose
To become aware of how smell affects individuals

To use smell to stimulate the imagination

To explore differences in people's responses to smell

To work imaginatively

Participants and Space
Any number, a large space.

Activity
Have each person work with an interesting smell. More than one person can use the same one.

Use various media to express response to smells. Work with color (paints, crayons, pastels). Create a movement piece; make up a story that is written or acted out; compose some music using real instruments or sounds. When finished, share responses with the total group. Work with several smells and more than one medium. Have the whole group discuss how the stimulus helped create.

Suggestions
Encourage people to work in media with which they are unfamiliar. If one person always writes, suggest paints or clay. Note how the same smell elicits different response in different media. Work individually and in a group. Conduct as much of this activity as possible non-verbally.

Questions

Is smell a good stimulus for you? Why or why not?

How do the ideas from working with smell differ from ideas of other senses, such as vision or touch?

Why do people respond differently to the same smell?

Do people tend to find some smells in particular good or bad?

Do you tend to associate certain places with certain smells?

What effect does this activity have on your perceptions in daily living?

SOUND STORIES (II)

Purpose

To use sound to stimulate ideas

To become more aware of sound

To work cooperatively

To respond imaginatively to sound

Participants and Space

Small groups with space in which to move.

Activity

Each person in the group should have his/her own sound. After listening to each other's sounds, compose a sound story by putting together the sounds as if they were words. Whenever possible, tape the story.

Sound stories can be used in various ways. A group can respond non-verbally, creating a movement piece to accompany the sounds. Or, a group can use words and mime and tell a story realistically (cellophane crackling sounds like eggs cooking, hollow boxes hitting the floor like horses galloping). Or, a group can paint, draw or sculpt their response. After all groups have finished, share stories.

Suggestions

Before sharing work, have one group work with another group's sound story, if taped. Emphasize the many possible responses, rather than whether a specific response is good or bad. Try reversing the process, and creating sound stories from paintings, drawings, photographs, sculpture, newspaper articles, and so on.

Questions

How do you decide what sound fits an idea or feeling?
What sounds do you like?
What sounds do you dislike?
Does each culture's music use the same sounds?
Do you associate certain colors with certain sounds?

ALBUM COVERS FOR SOUND STORIES

Purpose

To explore visual response to sound
To work cooperatively
To respond imaginatively to sound

Participants and Space

Small groups of people; space to work apart from each other.

Activity

Listen to a sound story, on tape if possible. Use 3-dimensional objects with a variety of shapes, textures, colors and sizes to create an album cover. Use cardboard as the base. Work non-verbally. The whole group should decide when to stop. Do not discuss ahead of time what should be done or who should do what. Share the covers by having each group look at all the covers and listen to the corresponding sound story.

Suggestions

Each group can use another group's cover, and create a movement or dramatic response to it. Have each person select the cover that is most interesting, and write how it makes him/her feel, what kinds of images are suggested. Have everybody bring in material with which to make covers. Locate this material centrally, so everybody can see what is available while listening to the sound stories.

Questions

What effect did working non-verbally on the covers have on you and the group?

Do you easily see movement in shapes, see images in sounds?

Is there such a thing as blank space?

ESTABLISHING ENVIRONMENT (II)

Purpose

To be aware of how environment affects people

To explore various responses in a fixed situation

To work cooperatively

To respond imaginatively to non-verbal cues

To maintain illusion created by the group

Participants and Space

Small groups; space large enough to move in and around.

Activity

Have each person non-verbally establish a physical environment. The person should repond to this environment individually, then develop how some imaginary person might respond. Explore how different responses to the same environment affect relationships. If one person is afraid, do the other members of the group jeer, comfort, ignore, disbelieve? Use gibberish or non-verbal sounds to augment feelings and response.

Suggestions

Try responding to the same environment in several different ways. If the first time you were afraid, later be courageous. If you ignored silliness, later indulge it. Pay attention to the allies that develop within a group, depending on which response is chosen. Use words and see how this affects the experience.

Questions

In this activity, do your emotional responses seem real or forced?

What does it take for them to seem real?

Have you ever noticed how people respond in environments such as restaurants, railroad stations, airports, doctors' offices?

What feelings or attitudes are expressed non-verbally?

Are these picked up by strangers?

What actions (non-verbal) of other people make you feel uncomfortable in a strange environment? Would they make you feel equally uncomfortable in a familiar environment?

Does this activity affect your perception in daily living?

ESTABLISHING ENVIRONMENT (III)

Purpose

To create new environments

To create and sustain imagined relationships

To work cooperatively

To explore possibilities in a fixed situation

To respond to non-verbal cues

Participants and Space

Small groups; space large enough to move in and around. It is helpful to have changeable levels (chairs, desks, boxes).

Activity

Non-verbally, in a small group, establish an environment. Explore possible responses to it and to each other. Find either an end or a stopping place. Be able to repeat the work.

Have each small group share its environment with the larger group. Then repeat a second time, and have those watching respond to the environment by contributing sounds (if a jungle, the cries of birds and animals); obstacles (if a school bus, something lying in the street); psychological effect (stand on a different level and stare at the group working). The point is not to disrupt the action, but to provide new stimulation within the context established.

Suggestions

Try adding words after exploring non-verbal possibilities. In order to prevent chaos, have those watching be selective about their contributions. If the group becomes disorderly, work in slow motion. Have those watching contribute both neutral and emotionally charged stimuli. (An owl can be hooting, or hooting in fear, which will have a different effect.)

Questions

How do you feel when your group receives new stimuli?

Do you anticipate things, or can you work spontaneously?

How do you feel when the stimulation is vocal, or physical, or psychological?

Do the other members of your group respond differently?

How does sudden change affect you?

How does working this way affect your feelings toward your own group and toward the larger group?

WORKING IN ALTERED SPACES (II)

Purpose

To explore the effect of space on feelings

To be sensitive to the effects of changing space

To explore the effect of people on each other in altered spaces

To explore differences in response to the same altered space

To work imaginatively

Participants and Space

Any number, with people working alone or in small groups; a large enough space to include varied working spaces. This is difficult for very young children.

Activity

Have people work individually in an altered space. After each person has worked, share responses with the group. Without speaking, have each person now work with a partner and explore the space that each had worked in alone. Share these new responses with the group. Discuss how feelings changed, what were the differences between the two experiences, and if people preferred to work alone or with others.

Repeat this activity many times under different circumstances, such as different types of weather, exams, toward the beginning of the year, close to vacation.

Questions

Are you aware of the factors that make you feel comfortable or uncomfortable in a particular space?

Does it make a difference whether you work alone or with someone?

Does it matter who that person is?

How can you make a strange space feel comfortable?

How can you make a comfortable space feel uncomfortable?

How does light affect your feelings about space?

Which do you prefer, day or night?

What effect does smell have on your feelings about space?

Can you feel space if you can not see?

ESTABLISHING IDENTITY (II)

Purpose

To become sensitive to cues telling who and what a person is and does

To learn which non-verbal signals a person gives and receives

To explore how people are affected by relationship

To work cooperatively

Participants and Space

Any number, any space.

This activity is difficult, and can quickly be reduced to chaos. Help young children work slowly and carefully. Limit the number of participants, starting with 3 or 4, until the group has enough experience and confidence to handle more.

Activity

Have one person begin an action, such as hanging drapes or writing a letter. A second person establishes his/her relationship to the first person while furthering the action. For example: the drape-hanger can be an interior decorator; the second person can be a member of the household. A third person, taking into account the established roles, then enters into the action, giving clues as to his/her identity. Those watching should note what is changed and what remains the same; how able people are to act their role, and whether people are really listening to each other. Those working should try to find a stopping place or ending, but may need help in the beginning.

Suggestions

Those watching can stop the work when they notice inconsistencies. Each group will need to try this activity several times before they can work effectively with each other. Group discussions help individuals understand how to improve their work.

Questions

In daily living, do you ever wonder who someone is?

What clues give you information?

Do you find this activity difficult? Why?

What effect does working this way have on you and the group?

If practice makes this activity easier, what is it you are learning?

WORKING WITH OBSTACLES (III)
Purpose
To improve kinesthetic sense

To develop spatial awareness and memory

To improve concentration

Participants and Space
Any number, depending on the size of the space. Supervise young children closely.

Activity
Divide into two groups. Have one group create an obstacle course with desks, chairs, other objects, and people (be more careful when people are used). The other group should study the course carefully, with eyes open, for as long as necessary. Then the members of this group should close their eyes and move through the course, trying not to bump into any of the obstacles. If the group is experienced, give a shorter time limit. The faster the time, the more difficult and dangerous the activity will become.

Suggestions
With more experience, add levels in space. Keep the volume down; it is very difficult to maneuver the course at high speed with loud background noise. In helping to develop spatial awareness, this activity develops a skill which prevents injuries when working in a darkened place, such as the backstage area during a performance. Encourage people with perceptual

problems to work at their own speed, without comparing themselves to others. No-one should feel pressured into going faster than his/her level of competency allows.

Questions

How accurate is your perception?

How accurate is your memory of the relative arrangement of objects in space?

When studying the obstacles before going through them, what do you look at and for?

How does tempo affect perception?

WORKING IN SOMEONE ELSE'S SPACE (II)

Purpose

To develop spatial awareness

To experience how pace and tension level affect perception

To work with concentration and cooperation

To work imaginatively

To think of ideas without self-censorship

Participants and Space

Start with partners, move to larger groups; space in which all groups can work comfortably.

Activity

One person makes his/her body into a shape. When finished, a second person finds some empty space defined by the position of the first person, and moves into it, without touching the person. When finished (this is established non-verbally), the first person finds a new space. On a signal from the leader both people freeze. Using action and (if necessary) words, think of an activity both people could be doing, such as playing tag. If both people have different reactions at the same time, try to use both. Repeat this activity with several different people.

Suggestions

Share work with the group, so different possibilities can be demonstrated. With experience, have the group work in 3's and 4's. Experiment with the effect of tension levels by having the partners do one activity with little, then great, degrees of tension. If some people tend to talk a lot, have them work nonverbally. Afterwards, discuss problems, stimuli for new ideas, and general responses.

Questions

Why are some people harder or easier to work with than others?

What movements give you ideas?

What do you do when you can't think of anything to do?

How would this activity change if you added physical contact?

What problems arise when you work with more than two people?

How do you feel about personal space: do you like working so close to another person?

GROUP LEAN

Purpose

To explore group balance

To improve kinesthetic sense

To improve sense of timing and rhythm

To experience supporting and being supported simultaneously

Participants and Space

Any even number of people, groups of 12 work well; space large enough for all those working to move around freely. Very young children will find this activity difficult.

Activity

Have the group form a circle, holding hands, and count off 1, 2, 1, 2, until everyone has a number. (If there is an uneven number of people, have someone step out, and switch places after the activity has been tried once.) Number 1's start by leaning out, number 2's by leaning in. Take four counts to lean, four counts to come to center, four counts to lean in the opposite direction, and four to come to center again. Have the leader give the group four counts before starting, to set the shared pace. The first few times, the leader should count out loud; then each person should keep time silently. The closer together the group is, the easier it is to lean. Try holding hands then wrists, to see which works better. Work for a sense of folding and unfolding, as in a flower.

Suggestions

Share images which this activity brings to mind. Try to balance weight and size so that small people are not next to large ones. In the beginning, work slowly and not too closely. Try to be aware of, and release, all unnecessary tension. Try working with eyes closed, and with sounds. If mats are available, work on knees.

Questions

How do you feel doing this activity?

How does working with sound alter it?

What happens when you work with your eyes closed?

Can you feel areas of too much tension in yourself? Can you release tension while working?

How does it feel to support someone while you are being supported?

Can you think of similar activities that the group might try?

SHARING IMAGINARY OBJECTS

Purpose

To improve powers of observation and concentration

To work cooperatively with imagination

To create and sustain illusion

Participants and Space

Any number, any space.

Activity

Working in partners, have one person start to shape an object to be used. As soon as the partner understands what the object will be and how it will be used, both should finish making it and begin using it. For instance, if the first person is creating a ball, when the roundness is established, the partner should finish making it, and non-verbally suggest ways to play with it. Use sounds but not words. When finished, switch roles. Repeat the activity with other partners. Work with three if there is an odd number of people.

Suggestions

Use the imaginary object as the basis of an improvisation that will develop a relationship between the partners. Discuss afterwards where and how the shaping took place, and how they feel about the experience.

Questions

How do you decide what object is being made?

How do you communicate non-verbally, without grunting or gesturing?

Can you explore a variety of feelings that creating and using an object might evoke?

What do you use to stimulate an emotional response? Do the emotions seem real or phoney?

How does your partner's response affect your work?

Why are some people easier to work with than others?

Why are some objects harder to make or figure out than others?

What helps make an imaginary object seem real?

How do you feel about working non-verbally? How does it affect your powers of concentration and observation?

PHYSICALIZING SENSORY IMAGES

Purpose

To create sensory images

To explore physicalization of images

To work imaginatively

To work cooperatively

Participants and Space

Any number, any space.

Activity

Divide into small groups of 4 or 5. Have each group think of an image (eating an ice cream cone from the bottom on a very hot day, or the sea breaking over rocks and then receding). Write down all the images so they can be shared. Have each group explore many images. Share the results of these physicalizations.

Suggestions

After sharing work, those watching might offer qualifications (how would it be if the ice cream was eaten by an ant, or by a giant? How would the sea move during a storm; at high tide or at low tide?) Those watching could contribute sound effects, could alter the physical space. Connect various images and create a series. Change the dynamics and the focus and note the effects. What would happen if the group working used flashlights and the room were dark? If they worked under a sheet or parachute? It is not important to guess the image, but to communicate the feelings evoked by it.

Questions

How do you think of images? Do images come to mind more easily at certain times and under certain circumstances?

What environment supports the evocation of images?

Do you see images in abstract painting, in cloud formations, in patterns of wind on water?

What feelings are most stimulated by imagery?

Does a realistic description or depiction (words or drawing) support and stimulate images for you or do you prefer less realistic stimuli?

ACTION, REACTION

Purpose

To work with actions that demand response

To explore non-verbal communication

To feel comfortable with absurdity

To work non-literally

Participants and Space

Any number, any space.

Young children may find this activity difficult, and should be supervised.

Activity

Work in partners. Have one person make a movement or sound that requires a response from the partner. The partner responds, and initiates a new activity which requires its own response.

Explore a variety of dynamics, directions, levels, rhythms. Try not to mime or "make sense"; the point is to explore activities which do and do not seem complete, which do or do not call for a response. Work with various partners before coming together as a group to share experiences.

Suggestions

Observe a conversation between people whose words you cannot hear, noting the level of physicalization in the interaction. Analyze what makes you think they are interested or disinterested in each other's argument. Watch a television program without the sound, and see what you can infer about the people involved. Have someone else watch it at the same time with the sound, and compare, to see if your observations were correct.

Questions

What motions, sounds, or body positions do you feel a need to respond to? What turns you away?

Why are some people more difficult to work with than others?

Can you tell someone he/she is difficult to work with, and thus improve communication?

Can you discuss problems of working with your partner? How does this affect the partner's response?

PHYSICALIZING RESPONSE

Purpose

To explore non-verbal communication

To explore the difference between what one thinks one is communicating, and what others think is being communicated

To physicalize feelings openly

To work with sensitivity and connection to other people

Participants and Space

Any number, any space.

This activity is difficult, but not impossible, for young children. The leader must work with the whole group, and not divide up into pairs.

Older people feel self-conscious doing this activity. Do not attempt it until the members of the group feel confortable with each other and have developed physical and emotional trust in each other.

Activity

Work in pairs. Have one person non-verbally try to communicate a feeling, idea or attitude which will evoke a response. The partner should respond openly to the first person's action. Discuss the difference, if any, between what the first person wanted to communicate and what the second person understood, when the work is finished. Avoid gestures such as shoulder shrugging and pointing. When everybody has worked with several different partners, discuss work with the group, comparing intentions and responses. People can share work if desired.

Suggestions

If the group is shy and unable to start, begin with activities such as *tangling* or *follow the leader*. Have people volunteer to demonstrate if the group does not understand. Repeat this activity at different times and occasions; most groups have difficulty with it the first few times. With experience, the second person can respond to the first, and then initiate a new activity, calling for a response from the first person.

Questions

Was the activity difficult, embarrassing, challenging for you? Why?

What clues tell you the response to give another person?

What ideas and feelings are easy, which are difficult to relate?

How can you help your partner?

When are words needed?

ROLE-PLAYING

There is a great deal written on the subject of role-playing; its effect on those who participate and those who watch. For our purposes, role-playing is useful because it provides us with a chance to see ourselves as other see us. Group role-playing provides insights into how people live, and what factors are influential. The leader must be careful not to use role-playing as psychodrama, an activity to be led only by professional psychologists. Do not try to analyze; let the experience speak for itself, and questions or comments will arise naturally when the group is ready. The following incident illustrates how role-playing can work.

I was doing role-playing exercises with a group of 12 to 14-year-old boys in an inner city school. I divided them into groups of three to six, and told them to create a short play based on something they had experienced or seen. One of the groups came up with the following. There were three boys playing in the street, despite warnings from an older man (the father of one of the boys), who kept saying that the street was a dangerous place to play. The boys ignored the man's warnings, and continued to play, mimicking the man's speech and movements. After the old man had left, a fourth boy, representing a car, ran over one of the boys and killed him. The car then turned into the driver, who screamed at the boys for playing in the street, called the police, and went to notify the father. When the boy playing the old man heard about his son's death, he began to cry in earnest, paying no attention to the boys acting as policemen. The police then turned into a funeral director and pall-bearers, and a burial service was held. The boy playing the father continued to weep. After the service, the boys, acting as mourners, led the father home and tried to comfort him. They suggested that the city make a play street out of the street where his son was killed, and name it after his son. The play ended with a scene of the old man, left alone, rocking in a chair and reminiscing out loud about his son.

All the people watching the work were totally involved. When the play was over, no-one moved or spoke. The boy who had played the father seemed exhausted. The group agreed that no-one else wanted to work, so we waited until the next session to continue.

My curiosity had been aroused, so I called the boys' homeroom teacher to relate what had happened. The teacher then explained to me that the boy who had played the father had seen his best friend killed by a car, and had been unable to deal with the incident, acting belligerently, then dejectedly in turn. A few days later the teacher called me back to say that the role-playing session had helped the boy; he seemed more relaxed and in better contact with himself and others. The play had enabled him to show his emotions in a safe way, without jeopardizing his image (boys should not cry), and had helped him deal with his guilt and his grief.

Purpose

To develop perspective about one's self and others

To explore alternatives

To see situations through other people's eyes

To be sensitive to different people's reactions and feelings

Participants and Space

Any number, large space.

This activity can be used to explore solutions to difficult problems of the group as well as individuals. To demonstrate, have a volunteer (it could be the leader) recount an incident to which the group could find a satisfactory solution.

Young children can use role-playing to explore occupations, situations with parents and teachers, and peer relationships.

Activity

Divide the group into small groups, letting people work with those they feel comfortable. Select an incident or situation to explore. In the beginning, when learning the technique, avoid incidents in which specific people may be recognized. Have each member of the group develop a specific role, and relate to the total situation through the character's eyes. It is interesting when everyone works on the same situation and then shares results. In the beginning, have one group work at a time, while the others watch to see how the work is developed. When sharing, try to avoid judgemental comments which put people on the defensive. Focus on understanding something from another person's point of view.

Suggestions

As the group gains experience, use difficult experiences from every-day life, having people assume all the key roles. Encourage questions such as, "How might this person respond?" rather than asking "Why did you . . . " When the comments do not deal with right or wrong, good or bad, it will be easier to accept "good" and "bad" as integral parts of any individual. A person cannot be defensive and open to change at the same time.

Questions

How do you feel watching other people act out your situation?

Does watching others in your situation give you a different perspective?

Do you feel the need to defend yourself even when you did not like something you said or did? Why?

What insights does this activity give you about yourself?

Does this way of working have any effect on your daily living?

What does it take to be able to work openly in this activity?

MAKING MASKS WITH THE FACE (I)

Purpose

To explore how changing the face can affect the total body image

To use the changed face to stimulate ideas

To work imaginatively

Participants and Space

Any number, any space; mirrors if possible.

Activity

Using your own features, create a mask for your face. Work with a mirror until you can maintain the new facial expression for a few minutes. Alternate this activity with others to relieve fatigue of the facial muscles. Try making a variety of face masks. Explore how the mask changes the way the body moves. Move in the new way the mask suggests; try different motions and actions, walking, sitting, crossing a narrow bridge, and so on.

Suggestions

Once you can maintain the facial mask and have evolved a complementary body movement, interact with another person. Then interact with a variety of people. Establish a common activity, such as shopping in an open market, reading a newspaper, running for a bus, and have everybody try it. Have the group comment on the type of person you appear to be, what your occupation might be, your likes and dislikes.

Questions

How does your facial expression affect the rest of your body?
Can your face limit what the body could do?
If mirrors are unavailable, how do you remember your mask?
How do feelings affect your face?
Can you have one side of your face showing one expression, and the other side another?
How can you maintain a constant mask when your feelings change?
Have you ever seen Marcel Marceau's mime sketch, *The Mask*? (It is the story of a mask-maker who tries on various masks. The happy mask gets stuck, and he cannot pull it off. Finally, with his body crying and his face still smiling, he pries it off, revealing his real face which was crying with his body.)

MAKING MASKS WITH THE FACE (II)

Purpose

To explore how changing the face affects the total body image

To use the changed face to stimulate improvisation

To work imaginatively

Participants and Space

Any number, any space.

Activity

Create a mask with features of your face. Develop a body posture and way of moving that corresponds with the facial mask. Form small groups of 3 or 4 and create an improvisation based on the new characters. Before deciding the final sequence of events, explore what the characters might or might not feel and do. Use appropriate words or sounds. Try to keep the body and face integrated no matter what happens in the improvisation. Form new groups, and see how your character is affected by the new characters.

Suggestions

Make sure to rest the facial muscles sufficiently, and to stop whenever tired. Otherwise the facial mask will be lost without your knowing it. Keep the improvisations very short so the face and body movements can be maintained. If desired, use make-up.

Questions

When you change your face, are there some body positions that feel right and some that feel wrong? Why?

What would the effect on your character be if you added a new
qualification such as an injured leg, or limited vision?

Are there some masks which determine age, or can any mask
represent any age?

What effect do different experiences have on the face?

How much expression can you show without changing the
mask?

How does working with a real mask compare to using your
face as a mask?

What does your face do when you wear a real mask?

EXPECTED AND UNEXPECTED RESPONSES

Purpose

To explore paradox and incongruity

To explore the complexity of human response

To work cooperatively

Participants and Space

Any number with room in which to move; levels are helpful.
This activity is difficult for young children, but is possible if
the group works together to study motivation.

Activity

Have each person develop a character, with likes, dislikes,
habits, occupation, age, mannerisms. Develop one situation for
the whole group to use (a fire in your building; an impending
flood; threat of attack). Work in pairs, and show how each
character would respond to the situation and to the other
character. Change partners several times to explore various
responses. Work in small groups to explore how this affects the

action. Share work by having each small group do the activity while the rest of the group watches and offers suggestions for variation.

Suggestions

Have pieces of clothing and props available to aid in realizing characterizations. Use simple make-up, such as eye-liner, rouge, lipstick, eye shadow, and cold cream to remove it. Keep the situations simple so people can focus on the responses.

Questions

How would your character *not* respond? Why? Under what circumstances might this not be true?

Have you ever responded in a way that surprised you?

How do you decide what is a likely or an unlikely way for someone to respond?

What are the paradoxes you can see in yourself and your actions?

How common is paradoxical behavior? Is it desirable or not?

How does paradox make you feel?

MAKING UP GAMES TO EXPRESS FEELINGS

Purpose

To relieve the energy caused or accompanied by strong emotions

To find socially acceptable and safe ways of expressing emotions

To develop self control

Participants and Space

Number of people depends on the size of the room and the intensity of the emotion; the stronger the emotion, the larger the space needed.

Activity

In the middle of the room draw a large circle that is visible at a distance. Use chalk or make some mark to outline the area. Have one person step inside the circle and move as fast and furiously as possible, using appropriate sounds. A few at a time, the rest of the group should move across the room, watching out for the person in the middle. The people moving from one side of the room to the other can avoid the marked circle, but this is not nearly as interesting as trying to get through the circle without being touched by the "tornado." When the person in the circle gets tired, have someone else take over. Usually you have to watch out for others, which is very difficult when you are angry or upset; this game allows you to be as furious as you want (within the given boundaries), while everyone else has to watch out for you.

Suggestions

The people running through the circle may offer comments such as, "I feel like I'm running through a fire or war." Use these ideas to start a group improvisation. Encourage the group to invent their own games; it shows people how to work out personal solutions to general problems.

Questions

How do you feel when you are the "tornado" in the circle?

How do you feel trying to get past the "tornado" without being touched?

Do you like the feeling of you or someone else being allowed to have a space in which to move as violently as necessary?

How long can you sustain this high pitch?

What kind of energy do the emotions of anger, frustration, repulsion, pity, love, have?

Can you think of other games that could release emotional energy?

What do you do when you are very angry? How could you handle your anger now?

MAKING A WHOLE OUT OF PARTS

Purpose

To work cooperatively

To work imaginatively

To respond spontaneously to an action

Participants and Space

Small groups, a fairly large space. It helps to have boxes to stand on, ropes to pull, and so on.

This activity might be difficult for young children.

Activity

Have small groups work simultaneously. One person starts an action. A second person determines the place, time and activity of the first person, and joins in. Each person adds an element until the scene is completed. For example: one person is eating; a second person sits down at the table; the third person is the waiter, the fourth the maitre d'. When all members of the group have contributed, have them remember their action and relation to others around, so the piece can be repeated for the total group. Work non-verbally, but discuss after sharing.

Suggestions

If the group has trouble getting started, suggest a topic beforehand (an environment such as a forest or a haunted house; or different historical periods, such as the Civil War). Have people listen to and work off each other, paying attention to detail and complexity. With experience, the group can add attitudes (trees looking down on flowers, small animals trying to escape predators). If the group works well together, develop the work into an improvisation, with other groups composing a sound or musical score, painting a background or making props. Objects should be used in a variety of ways, regardless of their real use or shape.

Questions

How do you give clues to other people so they will know what to do? What clues do you look for in other people's work?

How do you make it clear the period is Civil War, not contemporary?

How do sounds affect your work?

How does it feel to take your clues from one person while giving clues to others?

EXPLORING RHYTHM

In music, a canon is a composition in which the same melody is played or sung by two or more voice parts at the same or a different pitch. The same idea can be expressed with rhythm.

Thus, two people can have the same time and distance to cover, but each person can use a different rhythm to cover it. For example, you could use a 4/4 measure, comprised of 4 one-beat notes (quarter notes) per measure. If a phrase was four measures long, several possibilities exist. As illustrated below, you could use 32 eighth notes (8 beats per measure), 16 quarter notes (4 beats per measure), 8 half notes (2 beats per measure), or 4 whole notes (1 beat per measure). You could mix the notes, though continuing to use 4 beats and the 4/4 measure.

4 measures:

⅛ notes	••••••••	••••••••	••••••••	••••••••	32 small, fast steps
¼ notes	• • • •	• • • •	• • • •	• • • •	16 average steps
½ notes	— —	— —	— —	— —	8 large, slow steps
whole note	—	—	—	—	4 larger, slower steps

In a canon, have one person mark whole notes, one mark half notes, one mark quarter notes and another mark eighth notes, and all should end at the same time and place. The following activity helps practice this in a simple way. With experience, the group can explore more complex ways of working with rhythm. To take up less space, work in a circle, with the person marking whole notes as the pivot.

Purpose

To explore rhythm

To experience using different numbers of beats to get to the same place at the same time

To work cooperatively and concentratedly

Participants and Space

Groups of four in a large open space.

Activity

Each group will work in a unit of four measures, using the same basic quarter note as the beat. Have each person practice the individual part by clapping the note value. The person with eighth notes will clap 32 times; the one with quarter notes will clap 16 times, the one with half-notes will clap 8 times, and the one with whole notes will clap 4 times. Everybody starts on the first count of each measure. After the clapping is understood, walk through the rhythms, according to the following diagrams. "D" is the pivot person, who changes direction but remains in the same place, at the center.

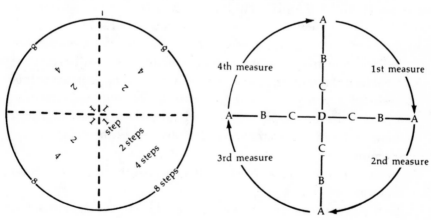

To make sure no-one gets ahead, have each group of four hold hands and tap the rhythms out with the feet. When these basic rhythmic patterns are understood, vary them by adding different sounds and body movements while the feet count out the rhythms. Give each person a chance to try each part, except people with learning disabilities, for whom this activity will be very difficult, and who should stay with the whole note part.

Suggestions

When experienced, change the circle to any shape the group desires. Remember that each rhythm must fit into the whole, so everyone must know when each new measure starts. Advanced people can work with syncopation; but this should not be attempted as a group until all members are fairly competent, since it can be frustrating if the group is not ready.

Do not try this activity when the group is worried, frustrated or tense, since it requires a great deal of concentration. In the beginning, have the leader establish a common pulse, but later the group should establish its own beat, faster or slower depending on its needs. Have the group suggest other ways of varying rhythmic patterns. This activity is a starting point, helping people understand how rhythms fit together. Have each group share work and discuss problems.

Questions

What other spatial arrangements of a group can be used for a canon besides a circle?

Can you work with your eyes closed, letting the person doing whole notes be the only one with eyes open?

How can this activity be made less frustrating?

The canon can be viewed as a metaphor for what?

What kind of cooperation is required in the group to do this activity correctly?

MAKING RHYTHM PUZZLES

Purpose

To explore possibilities of expressing feelings with rhythms

To work with cooperation and concentration

To maintain individuality within common group beat

To experiment with a variety of focus, level, tension and direction

Participants and Space

Any number, large open space.

This activity is difficult, and should not be tried until the group has mastered working with the canon.

Activity

Form small groups with space around each. Have each person develop a rhythmic movement pattern, using sounds that fit in a pre-determined group pulse. (Work with 4/4, or, if advanced, pulses of 7's, 5's, 9's.) To achieve variety, have each person work on a different level, with different degrees of tension, different points of focus and direction. The image of a puzzle containing different shapes within a single frame is analogous to the rhythm puzzle, containing various rhythms within one pulse. Add various sounds and movements if desired.

Suggestions

Work out puzzles that move in space as well as in place. Maintaining one rhythmic pattern, have each person explore variations of level, direction, and so on, to see the effects on the experience. Have those watching suggest images or ideas that the work suggests. If all groups are using the same pulse, have several groups work simultaneously, while others watch the visual images created.

Questions

How do you maintain your own rhythm when someone next to you is doing a different one?

How is the common pulse maintained when everyone is doing a different rhythm?

A rhythm puzzle could be a metaphor for what?

What can make this activity easier? More difficult?

PAPER BAGS AND CARDBOARD BOXES

The following activity developed out of a student's response to a teacher who said, "We will do creative activities from 2:00 to 3:00 on Friday afternoons." The student asked, "And what about all other times?" Realizing the absurdity of allowing one hour a week for creativity, the teacher told the class that whenever they had feelings, images or ideas that they wanted to explore, they should write them down, or find objects and put them in a box, which would be gone through on Friday afternoons. The box came to be known as "the feeling box." People began to put some objects in paper bags, meaning that they should be felt before being looked at. The box became a rich source of material as well as social comment; one day someone dumped a huge pile of mimeographed sheets, each with one sentence, with a note that read, "Two trees died for this!" Students used the box when they needed ideas for English compositions, social science and art projects. The box also became a gauge, reflecting how the students felt, and how their feelings changed.

Purpose

To devise a group barometer

To share feelings and ideas with a group anonymously

To release energy created by strong emotions

To use people's feelings and ideas as sources of stimulation

Participants and Space

Any number, any space.

If the group meets infrequently, have each person make his/her own box, to be shared with the total group periodically. The box becomes a special kind of diary, using objects as well as words to record and express feelings.

Activity

Have each person go the box and take a paper bag or object that is appealing. Using the object as stimulus, create a response to it with any medium that seems appropriate. If desired, work in pairs or small groups. Stress exploring the response to the stimulus, rather than presenting a finished product. Often the "product" can be a new object for the box. If the group wishes, share work.

Suggestions

The box should be handy to everyone at all times. If there is no room for a large box, use several small ones. Also have small empty bags available. Perishable items such as food should be put into the box only on days the box will be used. Periodically have the group look at the contents, talk about them, and discard those that are no longer interesting. This will give people a chance to examine their feelings, see how they have changed, and what new directions might be explored. When a person feels that an object he/she put into the box is no longer relevant, it can be removed at any time.

Questions

How do you find objects that represent feelings?

How does the process of looking for such an object, while you are experiencing strong feelings, affect the feelings?

Do other people's objects evoke the same response in you as it does in them?

How revealing do you find the objects?

Can you look at the contents of the box and get a good idea of how the group feels?

USING FOOD (II)

Purpose

To use food as a stimulus

To work imaginatively

To share responses and develop them into a group action

Participants and Space

Any number, any space in which there is room to move.

Activity

Divide into small groups of 3 or 4. Each group should have some food in a enclosed container, which each person should taste before seeing or smelling. After tasting, share feelings and ideas with the group so each small group can create a short drama, story, sound story, movement piece, mural or sculpture, exploring the group's feelings. When all groups have finished, share work with the total group.

Suggestions

Have everyone taste the same food at the same time. Specifically prepared foods, such as mashed potatoes dyed with food coloring, or shaped interestingly, are good experiences, since sight and even smell differ from taste. Encourage many responses. Do not always work with your first idea.

Questions

Are you easily stimulated by food? Why or why not?

Do you like paying close attention to details of texture, smell and taste, or do you not care?

Do you usually pay attention to what you are eating, or do you wolf it down?

If you have had a fight with someone while eating a particular food, do you continue to associate that food with that memory?

How does the environment affect your enjoyment of food?

Does preparing or eating food arouse feelings or emotions in you?

Do you find certain foods or beverages comforting or discomforting?

How are you affected by your family's or your culture's attitude toward food?

USING FOOD (III)

Purpose

To use food as a stimulus

To work imaginatively

To create characters from food stimulation

To become aware of memorable qualities of a food

Participants and Space

Any number, any space in which there is room to move.

This is a very difficult and complex activity, and should not be attempted until the group has experience in creating characters and role-playing.

Young children have trouble working from an abstract idea, so will need examples and help. The whole group should work together.

Older people may be inhibited emotionally, and not understand how to work. It helps to work with a few volunteers and let the rest of the group watch.

Activity

Recall how you felt when eating or preparing a certain food. Move the way these feelings make you want to move. Think what kind of person might move this way, and under what circumstances. Qualify your movement by the way this new character makes you feel. Use sounds and words when appropriate and unforced. Work with different people, noticing how you are affected by others' sounds and movements. Share responses with the group. Work with another person whose character or action relates to yours (sympathetic or anti-pathetic), and create a short piece. Non-verbally, find a stopping place or ending. Share work with the total group, revealing the source of the stimulus after the piece is shown.

The following description of two people's work will help clarify the purpose and process of the activity.

One person created a way of moving based on his feelings about shelling raw shrimp. Another person based his movement on his feelings about eating honey. As they moved, they were asked to imagine who they might be. The first man, moving erratically and tensely, said he felt like someone who was out of control. The second man, moving smoothly and relaxedly, said he felt like someone who had all the answers, totally in control. The two began to interact, though abstractly, adding sounds but no words. One of the group said they looked like a mental patient and an attendant. The two men accepted the suggestion, and began to assume roles: the tense one was the patient, the more relaxed one was the attendant. As the improvisation developed, they used phrases: the patient repeated "Help me," and the attendant answered, "You're fine, just fine." They repeated these phrases with different pitches and intensity. The patient tried to make contact, the attendant tried to remain uninvolved. The struggle between them was electrifying. When the patient screamed, "But I need you," burst into tears and clutched the attendant, those watching gasped. The attendant looked at the patient for what seemed to be a long time, and then opened his arms and began to comfort him, stroking and cradling the patient.

The people involved in this were not actors, nor were they attempting to act, for they did not begin the activity with an audience. The extraordinary work resulted from their intense involvement with each other, the concentration on each other's emotional states and needs. Though other groups were working simultaneously, they felt the intensity of the two men's work, and stopped their own to watch. After watching, the class was exhausted, as were the two participants. No one was able to move or talk. The work was not discussed until the following week.

Suggestions

Use other forms of expression: music, painting, sculpture, stories, poetry. Try this activity many times; it will call forth deepening levels of response. Avoid making judgements in group discussions. There is no need to "improve" a work unless it will be shared with outsiders. Respect original impulses and go with your feeling; no-one can tell you that you do not feel a certain way. Have the group ask questions suggesting possibilities that those working can explore or not.

Questions

How do you shape your feelings as you experience them, without censoring?

How comfortable do you feel revealing emotions to another person?

How do you feel working with a partner, as compared to sharing the work with the group?

What do you learn from watching other people's work?

What do you learn about yourself from this way of working?

When repeating your work, how do you remember what to do?

Can you repeat an idea or response without losing the freshness of the original impulse?

Does working this way affect your response as an audience member watching plays? If so, how?

GROUP STORIES, MOVEMENT AND MURALS
Purpose
To develop response to stimuli as a group

To develop ideas and work cooperatively

To be aware of different responses to one stimulus

To illustrate how parts fit into a whole

Participants and Space
Small groups of four or five; a large space in which to move.

Activity
Have each group develop a response to a predetermined stimulus, such as a school incident, a newspaper story or a familiar book. Whether the response takes the shape of painting, drama or movement, the process is the same. In painting, this might mean a mural; in drama, acting out a short story; in movement, a short dance. Develop these responses with little or no discussion and pre-planning. Share work. Then, as a total group, connect the separate parts to form a whole work. In the case of drama, if each story is complete in itself, use the

same theme, but tell each incident from a different point of view. In movement and art, fit the responses together to form a montage. If the pieces do not fit perfectly, this is all right. Usually, though, they fit, especially if the group knows in advance that the separate parts will be put together later. Discuss whether the total response is better or more effective than a single response, and why. Different groups can work in different media.

Suggestions

To make the activity more difficult, have each group develop only part of a response, which would then be joined with the other partial responses. (If the stimulus was protesting, the response could be just the image of waves breaking on rocks.) Parts could be exchanged between groups.

Questions

What effect does working without talking have on the experience?

What experiences did each group choose to highlight?

What ideas provide stimuli?

WORKING IMAGINATIVELY
WITH A VERY LARGE GROUP

Children often perform for adults, in school, recreational groups, or other institutions. Adults rarely get the opportunity to perform for children. The following activity makes it possible for children and adults to share performing, playing with and for each other without memorizing lines, sewing costumes or building sets. A core group is needed, providing one supervisor for every 8 or 10 participants. The supervisors will have determined a general structure and theme for the activity, and will also know how to work flexibly and spontaneously. It helps to have one extra person working a tape recorder or record-player, to provide appropriate music or sounds, and another extra person to provide some variety in lighting.

The following is an activity I devised when working with a group of about 150 people, which included three- and four-year-old children and their parents.

As the children and parents entered the room, each received a piece of colored yarn, about a yard long. They were asked to take off shoes and socks, and decorate themselves with the yarn for a trip to the circus. Those who started out watching but wanted to participate at any stage were free to do so.

We worked in a large room with an 8'x8'x3' platform in the center. Lights could be turned on, off, or half on and half off. There was a person operating a record-player who knew the experiences that had been planned, and who had also prepared a variety of sounds on a tape-recorder, which were soothing, exhilarating, strange. The activity started by calling "All aboard!"; everybody got onto an imaginary train behind two "engineers." The train traveled over rocks (formed by 4 adults), through tunnels (formed by older children), around trees (formed by adults and children), and was forced to halt in front of a huge mountain (formed by ten older children and adults). Since the mountain blocked the way to the circus area, everyone took out imaginary blasting equipment, and on a count of three blew up the mountain (much to everybody's delight). Once the mountain was moved out of the way, the train proceeded directly to the circus. Then the participants formed small groups of 10 to 15, with at least one adult and one leader per group. They pretended to eat lunch, and thought about what part of the circus they wanted to see. Because we were working with very young children, we gave each group a predetermined activity: lions and a tamer, jugglers, tight-rope walkers, and so on. We gave each person a piece of colored paper to help create illusion. The jugglers used the paper as balls and plates; the lions used it as manes, the tamers as whips; the tight-rope walkers used the paper on their heads to show precarious balance. No glue, paste, scissors or tape were necessary. After preparing their activities, each group took a turn "performing" on the raised platform, with appropriate music. The groups who were not performing sat around the platform and watched. After everyone had performed, the entire group paraded around the platform, including any interested spectators, until the music faded and the lights were turned on fully.

While people put on their shoes and socks, quiet music was played and the leaders gathered at the door to say good-bye. The whole activity lasted an hour.

One person was the conductor of the train and the ringmaster, and acted as a central control. For emergency use, a whistle was available, which would establish silence immediately. This was used only when hand signals for quiet could not be seen. Preparation included: 1) Deciding the main theme (train ride to the circus and the circus); 2) Props (colored yarn and paper); 3) Music and sounds (the train, circus acts, soothing exit music); 4) Assignments of roles and 5) General discussion, exploring what might happen, to anticipate ways of handling problems that might arise.

Purpose

To experience creative community drama

To work with people of different ages

To celebrate an occasion with drama, music and art

To create an informal play

Participants and Space

Any number, large open space; if possible, a raised area.

Activity

Depending on the age and experience of the group, choose a simple theme or action such as going to the circus, taking a boat-trip, going camping, visiting another planet.

Assign roles and responsibilities to the leaders. Practice solving problems that might arise. Establish control signals, which can be seen and heard, and introduce them to the group. Plan the overall structure of the experience, including how it will begin and how it will end. Plan how music or sounds will be used, how the lighting can be varied, and what props are necessary. Props should be simple, offer great variety, and be inexpensive. Avoid complications such as tape, glue or scissors which can be messy and dangerous. Decide on the central person in control; who it will be and how everybody will relate to that person.

Suggestions

To develop confidence and gain experience, start with a small group. A holiday such as Thanksgiving can provide a mood. A good rapport is essential between the person operating the music and the central person in command, so non-verbal signals can be communicated and correctly understood. Encourage everybody to participate rather than watch. Alternate energetic activities with quiet ones. Practice control signals with the group before starting. Prepare some warm-up exercises in case the group is shy or slow getting started.

Questions

How does this kind of dramatic activity compare with formal drama?

What is the effect of having everyone participate, at least most of the time?

What do you learn from working this way?

SECTION IV

The activities in this final section are based on a continually expanding range of source material. The stimuli for creative response are not only artistic or sensory; they include everything from newspaper articles to scientific theories. This will encourage the student not to limit the sources of stimulation, but to explore all kinds of possibilities. All the items selected here come from readily available sources, and students will find it easy to discover their own. Keep an empty scrapbook handy for stories, clippings, poems, photographs, art work and other images or ideas; also start a collection of tapes (sounds and music) and records. Instead of a bibliography for this chapter, I am including a partial list of sources for ideas.

These activities all share a common purpose, to stimulate imaginative and creative responses to an unlimited range of material. The poems should be read and responded to individually first, and then shared with the group, but all other material can be worked on by any size group. Each activity has only two parts, the stimulus and related questions. If the group is sharing work with a small audience, have the audience ask its own questions, and if desired, share the exploration. The question-oriented approach reinforces the idea of infinite possibility.

USING A FABLE
The Fable

The sun and the wind had an argument. Each thought the other was weaker. They asked the trees, the rain, the sky and the stones, who was the stronger? They could not get an answer. The birds suggested they hold a contest: whichever could make the approaching traveler remove his coat would be the stronger. They agreed. As the traveler drew nearer, the wind began to blow. The gentle breeze became a raging hurricane, but all the while the traveler held more tightly to his coat. Finally the wind gave up, and it was the sun's turn.

The sun began to beam down softly on the traveler. As the rays grew stronger, the traveler became hotter, and he soon removed his coat. The sun was truimphant.

Moral

Gentleness often succeeds where force fails.

Questions

What would happen if the coat was acted by a person?

What precipitated the argument?

Is gentleness always the best way? Why or why not?

How could you act out this fable using gibberish?

How could you choreograph this fable, using people as trees, birds, and so forth?

How could you use sound in this fable?

Could you paint a picture describing how the fable makes you feel?

What other stories might have a similar ending?

What stories would prove that force wins over gentleness?

How could you set this fable to music?

Could you make up a new story about characters like the sun or the wind?

How did the sun treat the wind after winning?

Under what circumstances might the sun have lost?

What other arguments might the sun and the wind have?

Do you agree or disagree with the ideas implied in this fable?

Could you invent your own fables?

POETRY (I)

he can not understand I have my own point of view

he thinks only his point of view is right, so he gets mad when I argue my point.

I say something—he says I should not say that, because it will get people mad—then he says something like I said and he says it's not the same thing

he says I keep repeating myself and I am not listening to him but he keeps repeating himself

he cannot understand I want to stand up for my view even
   though he has presented his view, because I will not agree
he says, what is the use of arguing over a point of view if
   nobody will switch
the use of it is to present each others' point of view

every time he gets in an argument he gets mad and it turns into
   a big fight
it always turns out that way
he always repeats himself in an argument and drags everything
   out forever and a day

(excerpt from a 12-year-old's diary.)

Questions
Who is "he"?

Which person do you identify with? Why?

What kind of incident might have provoked this?

How do you think writing this affected the person and the
   emotions of the moment?

What would happen if "I" shared this with "he"?

How could this piece be acted, moved or sounded?

How could you express your anger in the middle of experiencing the anger?

POETRY (II)
City
Children walk
with one
hand
out

to feel
what they are
walking
past.
A
city
is a bumpy
thing.

By Jane Stembridge,
from *I Play Flute*.
New York: Seabury Press, 1966.

Questions

How would you describe the place in which you live?

Would the description change if you could only feel rather than see it?

How would you paint a description of your environment?

How would you describe it if you could only use adjectives or colors?

How do the people in your environment affect your description of it?

Does the time or kind of day affect your feelings?

POETRY (III)

Class Assignment

Man, I don't wanna write no poem.
I mean, like, what's ta say?
Should I say, maybe, that Mrs. Perez
always smells of garlic
or that her kids

run up and down the halls
screamin'
til I think I'm gonna find me
the elevator shaft
and jump right in?
Ha, ha. How about this?
"The house is dirty,
the street is dirty,
I'm dirty."
Pretty good, huh?
Or maybe you'd like me to
write down that
I'm getting pretty sick of
talkin' to you
and that I just don't feel
like writin' down nothing.
I ain't got nothing pretty ta say.
A poem's gotta be pretty, ain't it?

By Marci Ridlons
in the *Arbuthnot Anthology of Children's Verse*.
Glenville, Illinois: Scott Foresman & Co., 1968.

Questions

Who decides what a poem should (or should not) be? On what
   basis? Do you agree or disagree?

Are there proper subjects for poems?

How does the poet decide what form the poem should take?
   What relationship is there between the form and the feeling?

How would it have been if the poet had chosen the essay form?

Can you write a poem describing your own feelings?

Look at some examples of concrete poetry. How does the word
placement affect the meaning?

POETRY (IV)

He always wanted to explain things
But no one cared
So he drew
Sometimes he would draw and it wasn't anything
He wanted to carve it in stone or write it in the sky
He would lie out in the grass and look up into the sky
And it would only be him and the sky and the things inside
him that needed saying
And it was after that he drew the picture
It was a beautiful picture
He kept it under his pillow and would let no one see it
And he would look at it every night and think about it
And when it was dark, and his eyes were closed, he could still
see it
And it was all of him
And he loved it
When he started school he brought it with him
Not to show anyone, but just to have it with him like a friend
It was funny about school
He sat in a square brown desk like all the other desks
And he thought it should be red
And his room was a square brown room
Just like all the others

And it was tight and close
And stiff
He hated to hold the pencil and chalk
With his arm stiff and feet flat on the floor stiff
With the teacher watching and watching
The teacher came and spoke to him
She told him to wear a tie like all the other boys
He said he didn't like them
She said it didn't matter. After that they drew
And he drew all yellow and it was the way he felt about the
    morning
And it was beautiful
The teacher came and smiled at him
What's this? she said Why don't you draw something like
    Ken's?
After that his mother bought him a tie
And he always drew airplanes and rocket ships like everyone
    else
And he threw the old pictures away
And when he lay alone looking at the sky
It was big and blue and all of everything
But he wasn't anymore
He was square inside and brown
And his hands were stiff
And he was like everyone else
And the things inside him that needed saying didn't need it
    anymore
It had stopped pushing

It was crushed
Stiff
Like everything else

This poem was handed to a teacher in Regina, Saskatchewan, Canada, by a grade twelve student. Although it is not known if he actually wrote the poem himself, it is known that he committed suicide a few weeks later.

Questions

How does this poem make you feel?

How does it relate to your experience in school?

POETRY (V)

The Poem as Mask

Orpheus

When I wrote of the women in their dances and wildness, it
    was a mask,
on their mountain, god-hunting, singing, in orgy,
it was a mask; when I wrote of the god,
fragmented, exiled from himself, his life, the love gone down
    with song,
it was myself, split open, unable to speak, in exile from myself.

There is no mountain, there is no god, there is memory
of my torn life, myself split open in sleep, the rescued child
beside me among the doctors, and a word
of rescue from the great eyes.

No more masks! No more mythologies!

Now, for the first time, the god lifts his hand,
the fragments join in me with their own music.

By Muriel Rukeyser,
in *No More Masks*, edited by Florence Howe and
Ellen Bass. Anchor Press, Doubleday, 1973.

Questions

If you have read *The Bacchae* by Euripides, how does this affect your thinking about this poem?

Do you feel as if you are a collection of fragmented selves? If so, how would you express this idea?

Do you wear a mask? Always, sometimes, never? What does wearing a mask do to the wearer, to those around him/her?

Do you ever consciously decide to "be what you are not"? How do you know what you are or are not?

Could you paint or move the notion of yourself with and without masks?

Could you describe yourself in a poem from your point of view, from others'?

How does society encourage or discourage the wearing of masks?

How vulnerable are you to the pressures of your own culture?

Are there times when you are more or less vulnerable? How does this make you feel? How can you express these feelings?

POETRY (VI)

True.
We look alike to you;
Green and shaped like hearts.

The wind blows down
And we blow down.
We whisper and get wet
As the rain starts.
But I can clearly see
Each one of us
Is as different
As each one of you.
Some are thinner
Paler
Longer
Tiny.
Patterns differ.
Some are fatter
Greener
Shiny.
Look around my home;
This tree.
You will not find another leaf
Compares to me.

By Karla Kuskin,
from *Any Me I Want to Be*.
New York: Harper & Row, 1972.

Questions

From whose point of view is this written?
Could you write this poem from the tree's point of view?
How does this poem relate to you?

How would you express this poem using movement? Paints? Sounds?

Could you write your own poem based on the theme of this poem?

Why does the author choose this form? What others might have been chosen? How would this affect the meaning? What is the relationship between the form and the content?

USING SCIENCE *What we perceive isn't necessarily what we see*

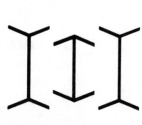

Which is longest?

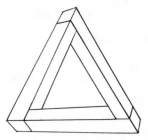

'Impossible' triangle

Questions

Do the three lines appear to be the same or different lengths?

Can you think of instances of having seen something which turned out to be different than what you first thought it was?

How can you tell whether your perceptions are accurate?

What kinds of illusions have you experienced?

How do people's perceptions differ?

If people perceive the same thing differently, how do you know who is right?

Describe a situation you and a friend saw to a third person. Are there differences in the way you relate it? If so, how does this make you feel?

What influences sensory perception?

What effect do exercises in perception have on drama and poetry?

Can you create your own optical illusions? Do other people respond to them differently?

What effect does sound have on silence? Eating on starvation? Confinement on freedom?

NEWSPAPER STORY (I)

"The Supreme Court ruled yesterday that the states have the right to require teachers to take an oath to uphold the federal and state constitutions. The action came in a brief order affirming a lower-court decision that a New York State law providing for such oaths of allegiance was constitutional."

Questions

If you were to use this article as the basis for an improvisation, who would the different characters represent?

Do you agree that oaths are reasonable?

How does this article make you feel?

What kind of people feel it is necessary to have oaths? Why?

How do (don't) oaths protect society?

What are some oaths you find reasonable?

What cultural conditions would make oaths seem necessary?

How did oath-taking originate? What might have caused people to deem them useful?

When did oath-taking in this country begin? Why?

Could you create a play based on the feelings of people who
write oaths and those who refuse to honor them?

NEWSPAPER STORY (II)

Recently an architect, who bought a lot in a small community,
designed and built a house for himself and his family. The community objected to his house, because it was very modern in
design, utilizing round shapes and multiple levels. The people in
the community sued him, and obtained a court order forcing the
architect to tear down his house.

Questions

Why would a house of different design disturb a
neighborhood?

What are the values that people who force a man to take his
house down might have?

What might these people have felt, to make them respond this
way?

How might the architect and his family have felt?

How might such an incident affect relationships within the
family?

Can you think of analogous incidents which you have experienced?

Can you use this story as the basis for a play, painting, sculpture, poem?

What was your response to this story?

Can you understand how or why the community felt
threatened?

What enables people to live comfortably with differences (in appearance, opinion, values)?

How do you deal with people who have different ideas or lifestyles?

How do you deal with people who challenge your ideas or lifestyle?

How do people learn to accept, use, enjoy the challenge of change?

What has made you re-evaluate and alter your own attitude, belief, dress, lifestyle? How does this experience of change make you feel about yourself and the people or circumstances that caused the change?

USING METAPHOR

Metaphors provide wonderful images which students can use to create improvisations, sculpture, painting, and so on. The image of a *prison* is one which is particularly powerful and evocative to people of all ages.

Questions

What parts of your life make you feel as if you were in prison?

How does being in prison, or the thought of it, make you feel?

Could you be freer in prison than out? How?

What associations do you get when the word "prison" is flashed?

What experience(s) have you had in prison (literal or metaphoric)?

How did you cope?

What are different kinds of prisons?

Do you know people who construct their own prisons?

How could you express the feelings you have about being in prison in a painting, sculpture, short story, poem?

Could you describe different kinds of freedom?

Why does the word "prison" evoke such powerful responses in so many people?

Have you ever been threatened with imprisonment?

If not, how might you have felt faced with this threat?

What would be grounds for imprisonment?

What are some other metaphors that are powerful and universal?

USING A FAIRY TALE
The Child Who Would Not Laugh

Once upon a time, there was a princess who would not laugh. Her parents gave her presents, brought in the court jester, had doctors examine her, all to no avail. Finally they offered her hand in marriage to any man who could make the princess laugh. Although many wealthy princes tried, they all failed. At last a poor but honest forester tried and succeeded, and they lived happily ever after.

One class updated this tale, and made the princess into an ordinary child (boy or girl) who is unable to laugh or smile. The parents try everything they can think of: presents, doctors, circus performers, lemonade sellers and musicians; nothing works. The problem of making the child smile can be solved in many ways. This particular group chose a child in the audience, who came up and whispered something in the unhappy child's ear. Soon the unhappy child began to laugh; what was needed was a friend. The grateful parents invited the audience to celebrate with them, and everybody danced to music.

Questions

If you were presenting this tale, how would you make the child laugh?

How would you end the tale?

Could you write songs to further the dramatic action? How and where would they fit in?

What other folk or fairy tales could you rewrite?

What criteria do you use for selecting other tales?

Could you perform this story without words? If so, what would the effect be?

Could you use this story as a source for another story? What kind of other tale could grow out of it?

Does the existence of movements such as Women's Liberation affect the way you feel about the original story?

Partial List of Sources

Museums
Theatre
Dance
Painting
Sculpture
Mime
Posters
Zoo
Circus
Rodeo
Carnival
Magic show
Sports
Political rallies
Personal experience
Vicarious experience
Group experience
Parks
Bus

Subway or train
Boat
Store
Dreams, nightmares
Weather
Colors
Time of day
Light
Sound
Music
Poetry
Literature
Film (animated and real)
Photographs
Magazines
Newspapers
Television
Radio
Overheard conversations

Overseen situations
Role-exchange
Parties
Fantasy
Strange spaces and places
Smells
Tastes
Textures
Sensory deprivation
    (no sight, touch, sound)
Flying
Junk
Shapes (abstract and real)
Frustration
Emotional energy
Temperature
Machines

. . . The end is not the end,
  but
The whole purpose of the beginning. So,
These leaves mix with earth to nourish others.
  And when snow is gone
They become the shade of another spring.

from:
A Poet and his Camera, by Gordon Parks.
New York: Viking Press, 1968.

Bibliographies

Bibliography For Chapter 1

[A] General Resources for further work

Ashton-Warner, Sylvia. *Spearpoint.* New York: Vintage Books, 1974.

　　　　Teacher. New York: Simon & Schuster, 1963.

Borton, Terry. *Reach, Touch & Teach.* New York: McGraw-Hill, 1970.

Brown, George Isaac. *Human Teaching for Human Learning.* New York: Viking Press, 1971.

Coles, Robert. *Children of Crisis: A Study of Courage and Fear.* Boston: Little, Brown & Co., 1964.

Deloria, Vine Jr. *We Talk, You Listen.* New York: Delta, 1970.

Dennison, George. *The Lives of Children: The Story of the First Street School.* New York: Random House, 1969.

Frankl, Viktor. *Man's Search for Meaning.* New York: Washington Square Press, 1963.

Hoetker, James. *Dramatics and the Teaching of Literature.* Champaign, Illinois: National Council of Teachers of English, 1969.

Jones, Richard M. *Fantasy and Feeling in the Classroom.* New York: New York University Press, 1968.

Koch, Kenneth. *Wishes, Lies and Dreams.* New York: Chelsea House Publishers, 1970.

Kohl, Herbert. *36 Children.* New York: New American Library, 1968.

Postman, Neil, and Weingartner, Charles. *Teaching As a Subversive Activity.* New York: Delacorte Press, 1969.

Reid, Virginia, ed. *Reading Ladders.* Washington, D.C.: American Council on Education, 1972.

Rogers, Carl. *On Becoming a Person.* Boston: Houghton Mifflin Co., 1961.

Silberman, Charles E. *Crisis in the Classroom.* New York: Random House, 1973.

Singer, Jerome. *The Child's World of Make-Believe.* New York: Academic Press, 1974.

Weitz, Shirley, ed. *Nonverbal Communication.* New York: Oxford University Press, 1974.

[B] New and Interesting Children's Books

Burch, Robert. *Queenie Peavy.* New York: Viking, 1966.

Donovan, John. *I'll Get There; It Better Be Worth the Trip.* New York: Harper, 1969.

Eckert, Allan W. *Incident at Hawk's Hill.* New York: Little, 1971.

Engdahl, Sylvia. *Enchantress from the Stars.* New York: Atheneum, 1972.

Fall, Thomas. *Canalboat to Freedom.* New York: Dial, 1966.

Forman, James. *People of the Dream.* New York: Farrar, 1972.

George, Jean. *Julie of the Wolves.* New York: Harper, 1972.

Hamilton, Virginia. *The House of Dies Drear.* New York: Macmillan, 1968.

Holm, Anne. *North to Freedom.* New York: Harcourt, 1966.

Hunt, Irene. *Across Five Aprils*. New York: Follett, 1964.

Hunter, Mollie. *The 13th Member: A Story of Suspense*. New York: Harper, 1971.

Kendall, Carol. *The Gammage Cup*. New York: Harcourt, 1959.

Klein, Norma. *Mom, The Wolf Man and Me*. New York: Avon, 1972.

O'Dell, Scott. *Island of the Blue Dolphins*. New York: Houghton Mifflin, 1960.

Robinson, Veronica. *David in Silence*. New York: Lippincott, 1966.

Speare, Elizabeth George. *The Witch of Blackbird Pond*. New York: Houghton, 1958.

Steele, Mary Q. *Journey Outside*. New York: Viking, 1969.

Walsh, Jill Paton. *Fireweed*. New York: Farrar, 1970.

Wojciechowska, Maia. *Shadow of a Bull*. New York: Atheneum, 1964.

Wrightson, Patricia. *A Racecourse for Andy*. New York: Harcourt, 1968.

[C] General Bibliographical Source

Bibliography of Books for Children. Association for Childhood Education International, 3615 Wisconsin Avenue NW. Washington, D.C. 20016 (1974 Edition: $2.75).

Personal Bibliography: Chapter 2

Ashton-Warner, Sylvia. *Spearpoint*. New York: Vintage Books, Random House, 1972.

Adler, Alfred. *Social Interest: A Challenge to Mankind*. New York: Capricorn Books, 1964.

Fabry, Joseph B. *The Pursuit of Meaning*. Boston: Beacon Press, 1968.

Ghiselin, Brewster, ed. *The Creative Process*. New York: Mentor Books, New American Library, 1955.

Howe, Florence, and Bass, Ellen, eds. *No More Masks*. Garden City, New York: Anchor Press, Doubleday, 1973.

Ibsen, Henrik. *Ghosts and Three Other Plays*. Garden City, New York: Anchor Press, Doubleday, 1966.

Kaufmann, Walter, ed. *Existentialism from Doestoevsky to Sartre*. New York: Meridian Books, 1956.

Klagsbrun, Francine, ed. *The First Ms. Reader*. New York: Warner Paperback Library, 1973.

Koestler, Arthur. *The Act of Creation*. New York: Dell Publishing Co., 1964.

Lahr, John, and Price, Jonathan. *Life-Show*. New York: Viking Press, 1973.

Lessing, Doris. *The Golden Notebook*. New York: Simon & Schuster, 1962.

Rosenberg, Harold. *Act and the Actor.* New York: World Publishing Co., 1970.

Ruitenbeek, Hendrik, ed. *The Creative Imagination.* Chicago, Ill.: Quadrangle Books, 1965.

Schachtel, Ernest G. *Metamorphosis.* New York: Basic Books, 1959.

Toffler, Alvin, ed. *Learning for Tomorrow.* New York: Random House, 1974.

Trumbo, Dalton. *Additional Dialogue.* New York: Evans and Co., 1970.

Watts, Alan. *The Wisdom of Insecurity.* New York: Vintage Books, 1951.

Weiss, Paul. *Nine Basic Arts.* Carbondale, Illinois: Southern Illinois Univ. Press, 1961.

Woolf, Virginia. *To the Lighthouse.* New York: Harcourt, Brace & World, 1927.

Bibliography for Chapter 3

Arbuthnot, May Hill, ed. *The Arbuthnot Anthology of Children's Literature.* Glenville, Illinois: Scott, Foresman and Co., 1971.

Bentley, William G. *Learning to Move, Moving to Learn.* New York: Citation Press, 1970.

Blackie, Pamela; Bullough, Bess; and Nash, Doris. *Drama.* New York: Citation Press. 1972.

Burns, Elizabeth. *Theatricality.* New York: Harper Torchbooks, 1972.

Cemrel, Inc. *The Aesthetic Education Program.* New York: Viking Press, 1973.

Cheifetz, Dan. *Theatre in My Head.* Boston: Little, Brown & Co., 1971.

Feldman, Edmund Burke. *Becoming Human Through Art Aesthetic Experience In the School.* Englewood Cliffs, N.J.: Prentice Hall, 1970.

Gerhardt, Lydia. *Moving and Knowing.* Englewood Cliffs, N.J.: Prentice Hall, 1973.

Gillies, Emily. *Creative Dramatics for all Children.* Association for Childhood Education International, Annual Bulletin Order, 1972–1973.

Hall, Edward T. *The Hidden Dimension.* New York: Doubleday, 1966.

Hodgson, John, and Richards, Ernest. *Improvisation.* London: Methuen & Co., University Paperback Drama Book, 1966.

Holt, John. *How Children Learn.* New York: Pitman Publishing Co., 1964.

Karl, Frederick R., and Hamalian, Leo. *The Existential Imagination.* Greenwich, Conn.: Fawcett Publications, Inc., 1963.

King, Nancy. *Theatre Movement: The Actor and His Space.* New York: Drama Book Specialists, 1971.

Langer, Susanne K. *Problems in Art.* New York: Charles Scribner's Sons, 1957.

Lee Dorothy: *Freedom and Culture.* Spectrum Books.

Leonard, George. *Education and Ecstasy.* New York: Delacorte Press, 1968.

Linderman, Donald W., and Herberholz, David W. *Developing Artistic and Perceptual Awareness.* Dubuque, Iowa: William C. Brown Co. 1970.

Lowenfeld, Viktor. *Creative and Mental Growth.* New York: Macmillan, 1947.

Lowndes, Betty. *Creative Movement and Drama for Children.* Boston: Plays Inc., 1971.

Maslow, Abraham H. *Toward a Psychology of Being.* Princeton, N.J.: Van Nostrand, 1962.

McLuhan, Marshall, and Parker, Harley. *Through the Vanishing Point.* New York: Harper & Row, 1968.

Mearns, Hughes. *Creative Power: The Education of Youth in the Creative Arts.* New York: Dover, 1958.

Neihardt, John. *Black Elk Speaks.* New York: Pocket Books, 1972.

Percival, Rachel, and Gray, Vera. *Music, Movement and Mime for Children.* London: Oxford University Press, 1962.

Reid, Virginia, ed. *Reading Ladders for Human Relations.* Washington, D.C.: American Council on Education, 1972.

Richards, M.C. *Centering.* Middletown, Conn.: Wesleyan University Press, 1962.

Romney, A. Kimball, and DeVore, Paul L. *You and Others.* Cambridge, Mass.: Winthrop Publishers, Inc., 1973.

Smith, James A. *Creative Teaching of the Creative Arts in the Elementary School.* Boston: Allyn & Bacon, Inc., 1967.

Thompson, William Irwin. *At the Edge of History.* New York: Harper Colophon Books, 1972.

Toffler, Alvin, ed. *The School-House in the City.* New York: Praeger, 1968 (N.B.: The article, "Alternatives to Urban Public Schools," by Kenneth B. Clark).

Turner, Margery J. *New Dance.* Pittsburgh, Penn.: University of Pittsburgh Press, 1971.

Van Hooft, Gordon E. *The Humanities: A Planning Guide for Teachers.* Albany, New York: New York State Education Department, Bureau of Secondary Curriculum, 1966.

Way, Brian. *Development Through Drama.* London: Longman, 1967.

Acknowledgements

One of the best parts of writing a book is the chance to thank, publicly, the people who have contributed to its formulation. Although I cannot thank by name all the teachers, students, and parents who tested and commented on my work, I do realize the important part they played, and thank them for it.

Every author needs a few special people who can be relied on to say what they think, even if it means more testing and writing. I would like to express my gratitude to:

Phyllis Conner and Phyllis Wynn, two teachers who have worked closely with me from the very beginning; Dr. Wesley Carlson, principal of Hillside School in Hastings-on-Hudson, who developed and is using an Arts-centered Curriculum; Richard M. Jones, whose comments and book, *Fantasy and Feeling in Education* pointed me in my present direction; Aileen Robbins Friedman, whose enthusiastic and supportive editing helped me continue writing long after I was sure that I had finished; Ralph Pine, who helped me find the center; Dorothy Louise, who has been colleague, critic and friend; Finn Hannover, whose loving "spontaneity" continues to nourish; and my parents, Ruth and Irving Rubin, whose love survived every test.

Photo credits:

p. 14 Tom Sherman; p. 24 Tom Sherman; p. 48 Tom Bethall; p. 50 Tom Sherman; p. 57 John Kaplan; p. 62 Patricia MacKay; p. 70 Tom Bethall; p. 77 Tom Bethall; p. 88 Tom Bethall; p. 100 Patricia MacKay; p. 109 Patricia MacKay; p. 114 Tom Bethall; p. 147 Tom Bethall; p. 161 Tom Sherman; p. 167 Patricia MacKay; p. 181 Patricia MacKay; p. 192 Tom Bethall; p. 219 Patricia MacKay; p. 235 John Kaplan; p. 310 Tom Sherman.